I0062030

The Absolutely Unbreakable Rules of IT Service Delivery

How to Manage Your IT Consulting Business to Maximize Customer Service, Profit, and Employee Culture

By Karl W. Palachuk

Published by

Great Little Book Publishing

Sacramento, CA
www.GreaLlittleBook.com

Great Little Book Publishing
Sacramento, CA

The Absolutely Unbreakable Rules of IT Service Delivery: How to Manage Your Business to Maximize Customer Service, Profit, and Employee Culture by Karl W. Palachuk

Copyright © 2020, 2026 by Karl W. Palachuk

All rights reserved. No part of this book may be used, reproduced, or distributed in any manner whatsoever without written permission.

This content is not available for artificial intelligence (AI) training. The author reserves all rights for AI training use.

No generative AI was used in the creation of this work.

ISBN 978-1-942115-71-7 (paperback)
ISBN 978-1-942115-67-0 (ebook)
ISBN 978-1-942115-68-7 (pdf)

Some pieces of this book were previously published in my blogs at blog.smallbizthoughts.com and relaxfocussucceed.com/blog. www.greatlittlebook.com

The Absolutely Unbreakable Rules of IT Service Delivery

How to Manage Your Business to Maximize Customer
Service, Profit, and Employee Culture

Karl W. Palachuk

Table of Contents

Your Downloadable Content

This book includes a few downloads that you will find very helpful.

If you purchased this book from Great Little Book Publishing, you should have received a download link when your purchase was completed. If you have problems finding this, email karl@karlpalachuk.com.

If you lost that or purchased from Amazon or another reseller, you can register at
AbsolutelyUnbreakableRules.com or
greatlittlebook.com.

Your feedback is always welcome.
– Karl P.
– karl@karlpalachuk.com

Introduction

This book started out as a one-page handout on my bulletin board. It was just a few simple "rules" about how we achieved and maintained success within our IT service business. It contained simple phrases such as, "Prioritize everything," and "Slow down, get more done."

The phrases were simple and easy to remember and repeat. But each of them also represented a philosophy about business that really did affect the way we operated.

And, I'm sure you can guess, they reflected the way I (the owner) wanted my company to show up for our clients. The rules either addressed how we delivered service, or how our internal processes kept us headed in the right direction.

Notice that "The customer is always right" is not on the list. Why? Because everyone knows that's not true. You have to be in business about one week to learn that customers are frequently wrong, or would make bad decisions if we didn't help them to make better decisions.

Over time the list grew, and the font size got smaller. At times, the list included several related items (e.g., rules for getting prepaid for hardware, monthly services, projects). Later, related items were combined into larger, more universal rules.

Eventually, I developed a presentation entitled, *The 25 Absolutely Unbreakable Rules of Service Delivery*. Unfortunately, it was hard to do justice to that presentation in less than two hours. But having fleshed out the philosophy behind each rule, that became the basis of this book.

I started my first business in 1995, and I've built a few since then. This book is based on twenty-five years of running and managing service businesses. Some of these are borne out of a desire to build my company culture in a certain direction. Others are the result of "lessons learned" from the mistakes we've made.

I decided to put these rules in book form for one simple reason: To help you benefit from the advice without making all the mistakes. So many times, people say things like, "I wish I'd known that when I first started." With some luck, folks getting started will read this and reach a higher level of success more quickly.

Good luck to you in your business. If you have questions or feedback, please email me: karl@karlpalachuk.com. I am honestly committed to your success, and I'll help you if I can.

I've been writing books since 1995. Well, let's be honest, I was writing before that. I've been *publishing* books since 2005. And while I've written books for the non-technical audience, my largest audience is IT professionals, mostly running their own small businesses.

So, I knew that a book on "Service Delivery" for a general audience would be missing some very tech-centric rules. Therefore, I've decided to create a very that is addressed to the professional IT consultant and includes several IT-specific rules.

And while the smart business owner of any business might find some value here, these chapters are unabashedly for the IT crowd. So, be warned, if you're not in IT, some of this may not make a lot of sense for your business.

Note: I make every attempt to honestly state what I believe and enjoy the freedom of writing whatever I feel like in my books and blogs. A mention of any product or service is not an endorsement.

As always, I thank you for your support and welcome your feedback.
- karl@karlpalachuk.com

Enjoy!
- Karl P.

The Absolutely Unbreakable Rules of Service Delivery

General Rules:
- Prioritize Everything
- Do not be interrupt-driven
- Slow down, get more done
- Know what you know
- The competition is irrelevant
- We only work with people we like

Rules for Client Management
- Define your ideal client—and go get them
- Don't have both sides of the conversation
- You're not responsible for every lost dog that shows up on your doorstep
- We can't care more about the client's network than they do
- Every client is on a service agreement
- Evaluate your pricing once a year

Rules for Managing Employees
- Hire an administrative assistant!
- Have a formal, detailed hiring process
- Hire slow; Fire fast
- Culture is built from the top down
- You can't control people, but you can control your processes

Rules for Billing and Finance
- Control billing and cash flow
- Get prepaid for everything you can
- All after-hours labor is billable
- It is not our responsibility to save the client's money
- You don't need to pick up every nickel you find
- If a client has a past-due balance, their service is cut off

Rules for Service Tickets
- Track ALL time inside your business
- All work is done on a service ticket
- Every ticket is massaged every time it's touched
- Every job has a scope
- Document absolutely everything

Section I
Successful Service Delivery

1. The Rules for Success

2. Success Is a Habit

3. Never Stop Learning

1. The Rules for Success

One of the most important things that you can do in your business is figure out why you're in business. If you haven't done so already, go read *Start with Why* by Simon Sinek. It's a truly spectacular book. So that's your first homework. It's also a good audiobook.

Sinek points out that nobody buys what you're selling because they need that product (service). The product or service is probably available from other companies. People do business with you because of *why* you do what you do. Think about the worst customer service experiences you've had: You were dealing, in almost every case, with somebody who doesn't know *why* their job exists.

They say things like, "We've always done it this way." Or, "We can't do that." Or, "Comcast won't give you a static IP." Uh, except when they do. These are people who are focused on trying to get by. They don't understand exactly what their function is in their company. So, fulfilling your need is not part of their equation.

Now think about why YOU are in business.

I've heard people define their company mission like this:
- "We provide the best tech support."
- "We provide the best, fastest service anywhere."
- "We provide supreme customer service."

Defining *some* guiding principle for your business is extremely important. But if you say, "Well, I just love software, I love installing software, I love patching software, and I like showing people how to use software," that's not *why* you're in business. That might be what you do, but it is not *why* you are in business.

I'm a firm believer that you should have guidelines that everyone in your company knows. The rules defined in this book are the guidelines that grew out of the service companies I have owned over the years. The one-page summary of the "unbreakable rules" grew from a habit I developed in my companies.

When I decided that something was important enough to become an unbreakable rule, I wrote it down and added it to the list. The title of this one-page document has changed over time. Eventually, it became a handout that we printed out and distributed.

Everybody who works for me has this on the bulletin board right next to their face, so that they can always see it. These rules are the company guidelines that we say to each other over and over. We repeat these things to each other all day, every day.

Some of these rules help us make money. Some of them keep our work standards high. Some build culture. All of them help us understand as a culture what's important inside our company.

As you build your list of unbreakable rules, you may not agree with all of mine. That's fine. Scratch off what you don't like, and add your own. You may have other rules for your life, or your business, that guide your success and personal fulfillment.

And while my audience is primarily IT service providers, many of these rules apply to any small business, or any service delivery business. For example, "We only work with people we like." That rule can dramatically improve your morale and culture. It's also an example of a rule that can increase goodness within your company but might cost you some money. You have to be committed to the belief that there are enough nice people in the world to keep your business afloat (there are).

The Giant Jigsaw

When I think of these rules, I imagine them to be a large jigsaw puzzle. All the pieces have to be there in order for you to create the whole picture. If you take something away, then you have you don't have the whole picture. I'm a firm believer that all these rules fit together.

When I sold one of my companies, the guy who bought it asked me flat out, "Will I make as much money as you did?" And I said, "Probably not, because I built this company on a series of unbreakable rules that all fit together. If you change anything, you will probably make less money."

For example, if you follow most of the rules but don't sign contracts, or don't get paid in advance, you will make less money. If you don't encourage clients to buy new equipment, you'll make less money.

Note: Of course, you may come up with a completely different set of rules. But please read through each rule in this book and give it a chance. While this list may not be perfect, I can promise that it's pretty good.

Some of you know the name Vilfredo Pareto. There's a function people in political science talk about called the Pareto optimal equation. Let's say you're negotiating something among many players. For example, consider several nations negotiating a treaty. The Pareto optimal position is the position in which every single thing in this equation is in its most advantageous position.

That does not mean that everyone gets what they want. But each need is maximized to the extent it can be, given the variety of needs. In other words, if you change anything, the balance is no longer *optimal* for one or more actors. So, "Pareto optimal" means everything fits together exactly and precisely, and each element balances the others.

Of course, you can't recreate my business. You probably don't live in Sacramento, California. You don't have my employees. You don't have my clients. You don't have my service offering or pricing. But you can create *your* set of rules that perfectly balance *your* business. I hope you'll find this book useful in figuring out what your rules are. Let this be a place to start.

Please note that I am extraordinarily opinionated about all of this stuff. That doesn't mean I'm right, but you'll see that I'm rather passionate about these rules.

2. Success Is a Habit

Some people who follow me on social media think I am an unreasonable boss, over-controlling, and that I ask the impossible from my staff. Those who have read my books tend to have a very different perception. I think the main difference is that those who dig in and read a book are more likely to understand the bigger, more complex picture.

I can honestly say that my employees have almost universally enjoyed working with me and the companies I've built. This is because I help them improve their skills, become more professional, and adopt habits that virtually guarantee their success going forward. And we accomplish this by focusing on proven practices.

I heard a very brilliant statement once that I have never found a verified source for:

> **You can't control people,**
> **but you can control your processes.**

This is SO true! You can't control employees, clients, vendors, sales people, or anyone else. But if you have good processes—and are committed to your processes—you can achieve anything.

And remember the jigsaw analogy. When everyone believes in documentation, standardization, and priorities, it becomes very easy to do very complicated things. You set priorities (which are standardized). You cross-train your team. You let employees manage themselves as much as they are able.

And this simple combination performs a bit of magic: You reduce "work in progress" and therefore everything moves faster. You get more work done because everyone is totally focused on the one job in front of them.

To some people, this seems like an impossible pipe-dream. But if everyone buys into the priority system, you can make it happen. And if everything is standardized and documented, and everyone is cross-trained, it can happen.

Think about your challenges. How do you get technicians to fill out their time cards? Process. How do you achieve flawless service delivery? Process. How do you know that every client system is working every single day? Process.

Here's an example of how process absolutely works: Sales. You might not think you have a sales process, but you do. Assuming you have more than one client, you have managed to "sell" your service several times. You might not have it documented or standardized in your mind, but you do *something*—and people sign a deal. What is that something?

For me, I love a very slow sales process. (Google: "Palachuk slow sales process" to see more.) Here's how it works. First, meet with the prospect and listen to every single thing they say. Do not talk about money. Change the conversation. Absolutely don't give a hint on pricing.

Second, you meet with the prospect and give them a report on what you learned last time. Basically, you're going to reflect back to them what they told you. If you can, build a vision of their future. What is the ideal? Where are you going, and what does it look like. Get feedback. Ask them if you can create a plan. Do not talk about money.

Third, you produce a rough plan. Get their feedback. Try to find out what's high, medium, and low priority. Try to get a budget from them.

Note: The key to success is to SLOW DOWN the process. Talk about the real problems. Talk about possible solutions. Talk about various options. Learn as much as you can so that you can give them a realistic proposal.

Finally, in the fourth meeting, you can propose your actual plan, with numbers. It makes no sense to talk money before this because you don't have enough information. And this is key: Until you've had a series of conversations, the client has no way to evaluate you . . . except for dollars.

Remember, the prospect has no idea what you do, how it works, or what it costs. They know nothing about your actual business. The only thing you have in common is money. You know what a dollar is worth; they know what a dollar is worth.

The sooner you bring up price—with no other context—the sooner they can compare you to someone else they saw online, or a commercial, or whatever. Remember the old sales rule: Whoever mentions money first loses.

Here's the point: Every single time I violate this process, I lose the sale. When I force the client to go through my slow process, they might buy. (I won't claim that they all buy.) But if I cut straight to the price, it's almost guaranteed that they *won't* buy.

I can't control people. But I can control my sales process.

Unfortunately, I have another example. Over the course of about ten years, I developed a fine-tuned hiring process. It was great at filtering people who weren't going to work out. It pre-qualified candidates before they showed up. And it guaranteed that they were a good contribution to our company culture once hired.

The single worst hire I ever made was the result of one big mistake: I violated my process. I short-circuited it. I hired the friend of a friend who I knew to be an amazing technician.

That hire was absolutely the worst technician I have ever worked with. In fact, he's the only person I have actually fired. Normally, I lay off people in order to down-size our operation. But I fired this guy with no qualms whatsoever. I wish I could hire him again just so I could fire him again!

Why did I go through that horrible experience? Because I didn't follow my process. The process worked: *I didn't!*

I say **success is a habit.** But, really, success is the habit of collecting and executing a series of successful habits.

This book is derived from twenty-five years of successful habits. Habits for running a business, habits for dealing with clients, habits for managing employees, and so on.

In my last book—*The Small Biz Quickstart Workbook*—I created a massive checklist of everything one needs to do in the year before and the year after starting a new business. When I talked about these massive to-do lists with business owners, I had to acknowledge that they already knew most of this stuff, or it was irrelevant.

For example:
- How do you get a business bank account?
- Do you need a tax ID?
- Where do you go to pay taxes?
- How do you hire someone?

If you've already gone through all that, the answers are pretty easy. If you and I started a business today, we would spend one minute talking about this kind of minutia. Why? Because these things are either so obvious or so un-related to our success that we know that they're not the juicy, good part of our new adventure.

You and I are going to create an awesome business to take over the world. Where we set up a bank account is the least important detail.

So, you see, at this most fundamental level, we know how to start a business and run a business. And we both know that that's not where the magic happens. Down the road, when it comes to branding, messaging, and service delivery, *that's* where we need to spend our energy. That's where the magic happens. That's where processes and procedures make us different from everyone else. That's where we excel while our competitors wonder what just happened.

Success is a habit because you can teach yourself to have the right conversations; to think in the right ways; to invest in the people who will make your business great. If you print out the Absolutely Unbreakable Rules, and post them on your wall, you can begin to follow each of them—or your variation on them. As each of them becomes a habit, it will make you just a little bit more successful.

As a Mandalorian would say, "This is the way."

3. Never Stop Learning

One of my favorite motivational speakers is Brian Tracy. If you ever run across his books or audio programs, make the investment. You won't be sorry.

And one of my favorite pieces of advice from Tracy is to listen to audio books. Whether you're driving around town, mowing the lawn, or just puttering around the house, you can literally go to school while going through your day, week, and year.

Perhaps the most important lesson I ever learned from my parents was to **never stop learning**. My father started and ran several businesses. In fact, after he had his first heart attack and could no longer do the hard work of a mechanic forty hours a week, he took classes and became an enrolled agent—a tax professional. My mother got involved in the business and she also became an enrolled agent in her 40's.

All my life, my first response to a challenge is to educate myself. I have an idea for a specialty food product, so I buy three books on the subject. I want to visit a friend in Thailand, so I buy a book on traveling in Thailand. I am called to be an expert witness, so I buy a book on how to be an expert witness.

This advice—Never Stop Learning—is not specific to the service industries. It really is good general advice for success in life. So maybe I should have left it for the Bonus Chapter at the end of the book. But if you're reading this, my guess is that you are already a believer.

The Internet: Blessing or Curse?

In many ways, the Internet has succeeded in its original purpose: Connecting massive amounts of information so we can easily link from one source to another. But at the same time, it has led to a massive amount of bad information, false information, and a very misleading understanding of many things.

For as long as I can remember, I have collected books filled with great quotes. Who said, "To thine own self be true?" (Polonius in Shakespeare's *Hamlet*).

But in the last chapter I presented a quote whose original source I cannot find. The reason I can't find it? The Internet has made it almost impossible to find the true source of many things.

I joke that almost anything ever said has either been attributed to Abraham Lincoln or Karl Marx—but it's pretty close to true!

The worst offenses are unintended. People are lazy, so a mis-quoted quote is attributed to the wrong person. And then it gets repeated. And then it goes on Instagram. And then it's repeated again and again, and eventually makes its way into the Congressional Record. And now it's true!

Here's a great example: Henry Ford never said:

"If I had asked people what they wanted, they would have said faster horses."

As far as we can tell, this misunderstanding comes from a misquote from "The Cruise Industry News Quarterly" in 1999. John McNeece, a cruise ship designer, said, "There is a problem trying to figure out what people want by canvassing them. I mean, if Henry Ford canvassed people on whether or not he should build a motor car, they'd probably tell him what they really wanted was a faster horse." (See https://quoteinvestigator.com/2011/07/28/ford-faster-horse/.)

You can see how easy it is to throw up an old picture and paste a variation of that on Instagram as a quote from Henry Ford.

The point is: Be careful out there! This is the tiniest example of the bad information you will find on the Internet. You need to do the research yourself. You need to choose sources you trust. And you need to dig deep.

Do not take advice just because it sounds good to you, or it fits with your preconceived notions about the world!

In the world of technology, I think we are naturally a little skeptical because many of us have been on "Newsgroups" and discussion groups for a long time. Anyone can show up and give advice, even if it's wrong and stupid.

One of the earliest cartoons about the Internet is from *The New Yorker* magazine in 1993. One dog is sitting at a computer and telling another dog: "On the Internet, no one knows you're a dog."

It turns out to be one of the most prophetic phrases ever put down in type.

So, it's harder than ever to get really good, valid advice on the Internet. But, at the same time, it's easier than ever to get lots and lots of advice on any subject you can imagine!

On one hand, you have to be committed to never-ending education. On the other hand, you have to make the effort to verify that what you're learning is true.

The Only Constant is Change

The IT industry moves very fast. But in the twenty-first century, every other industry moves fast as well. No matter what you do for a living, the industry has changed dramatically in the last five years. And the ten before that, and the fifteen before that.

No matter how far you think you are from technology, your industry has to constantly respond to new markets, new methods, new materials, and new fads. You can never stop learning. You can never just stand still and catch your breath.

As Robert Strauss says, "Success is a little like wrestling a gorilla. You don't quit when you're tired. You quit when the gorilla is tired." And we all know: The gorilla never gets tired.

Look ahead in your business. What will the world be like in five years? Can you even see that far? How about three years? Two?

As you look at your business and your future, you need to commit to constantly learning what's new and what's next. And don't allow yourself to feel beat down by the never-ending change. That's simply the way of the world.

Some people have always opposed whatever is new. But in the end, some new thing always wins over the old thing.

In one of Plato's writings—*The Phaedrus*—he presents a dialog in which Socrates makes an argument against writing. Yes: Socrates was opposed to the new fad of writing down ideas (circa 400 B.C.E.). He believed that the written word could not adequately express true knowledge.

So, be of good cheer! If you oppose some new technology, you are in good company. But be aware that some "new" thing will always replace the old thing. This new thing might not win the day, but that one will.

Over the years, I have met several business owners who said these words to me: "I just won't learn one more generation of knowledge." And those people then proceeded to retire or go bankrupt. In either case, they chose to exit the business rather than continue learning new things.

If you commit to being a life-long learner, your business need never die. If you resist the tendency to believe that you can hold back the progress of time, then you will constantly refresh your offering, refresh your business model, and refresh your business.

Choosing to learn means choosing to survive. Choosing to stop learning means choosing not to survive.

I know that's harsh, but I believe it's true.

Section II
Branding Is . . . Everything You Do

4. The KPE Way

5. Documentation and the E-Myth

6. The Way You Do Anything

4. The KPE Way

Hewlett Packard (HP) has a very famous set of guiding principles they refer to simply as "The HP Way." You can search that term and find a couple of different variations. These guidelines help employees, managers, sales people, and administrators to have a common framework.

The HP Way is short and to the point. But it guides how people treat each other, the role of profit in decision making, morals, integrity, teamwork, and more. And, of course, the title of David Packard's autobiography is *The HP Way*.

Early on in my first company (KPEnterprises), I started using the term The KPE Way. After all, there is a preferred way that I want employees to talk to each other and our clients. There's an emphasis on working with clients we enjoy being around.

Yes, money and profit are on the list as well, but profit needs to come in the context of a broader business strategy. As you'll see with the Unbreakable Rules of Service Delivery, our guidelines cover as much on the personal side of business as the practical side of service delivery.

There is also a connection between our "rules" and our standard operating procedures (SOPs). For example, we have an SOP on how to talk to a client on the first service call.

Your branding consists of everything you do. That means, the way you treat other employees is part of your brand; how you invoice is part of your brand; how you manage projects and work orders is part of your brand. Everything. Everything. Everything.

Here's a story that makes this point.

Two Electricians

Several years ago, I moved into a new-to-me old house. The electrical was definitely not up to twenty-first century standards. I knew I was bringing in several computers and other electronics, so I needed good, well-grounded electricity. I also wanted to install my hot tub, which requires a 50-amp dedicated 240-volt circuit.

So I called several electricians and got bids from three.

The first and second electricians were the two extremes with regard to branding. The first guy showed up in jeans. I told him what I wanted, which included two new 30-amp circuits plus the hot tub. He went around and inspected the circuit breaker box.

His recommendation: Well, the breaker box is completely full, but we can make it work. We'll replace a bunch of full-size breakers with half-size breakers. The 50-amp circuit is a bit of a stretch, but we can make it work.

He started talking about a $1,200 price tag. But as we talked more, he talked himself down to a $900 price. And eventually he said he could do it all for $800. I never asked for a discount. He literally talked himself down.

I had already checked out his contractor's license online so I knew he was licensed and bonded. In absence of any other information, I took his quote at face value.

Enter Electrician Two. Well, Electricians Two. Two guys showed up in uniforms. They put on booty covers to cover their feet as they entered the house. I told them what I wanted. They immediately demonstrated that they were miles ahead of the competition.

First, they took off some receptacle cover plates and looked inside to check out my assumptions about the grounding. They used a ground fault tester to verify that some outlets were not grounded properly. I had done this with a basic tester that simply said "ground fault." But they found some grounding, which means that incomplete grounding was taking place due to the wiring practices of the 1960s. The outlets had three-wire Romex, could be grounded easily, but were not grounded.

Second, they looked at the breaker box and said that it needed to be replaced. They recommended a 125-amp box, which could be gotten at a reasonable price. BUT it meant that they had to patch the wall where the old one came out. AND they would need to upgrade the connection to the electrical utility.

Third, we had a lengthy discussion about the wiring options for the hot tub. They recommended setting it up so that any hot tub we bought could be connected legally and safely.

Fourth, they said that we didn't have to add all the circuits I originally asked for. They recommended setting up three sets of outlets (as I wanted) but putting them all on one 20-amp circuit.

Fifth, they wanted to set up a ground system that brought the water heater and HVAC into alignment with modern code and safety standards.

Total estimate: $8,300. Yes. Ten times more than Electrician One.

The second electrical company got the bid simply because they started the engagement by doing everything the right way. I did talk them down about ten percent, but I had to do the talking.

Electrician One is very much like the consultant who starts with some false assumptions.

False Assumption One: It's all about the money. I don't want the house to burn down. I don't want a half-baked job. I don't know all the troubles that could come my way. And if the second quote was a few hundred dollars different, I might go with the $800 quote. But the difference was so dramatic that I had to take the higher quote seriously.

False Assumption Two: The buyer wants to make the old equipment last longer. If the old box had five open slots and was in great shape, things might be different. But it was already full and I didn't know what he had in mind to make it expand to fit my needs.

False Assumption Three: The buyer knows what's going on and what needs to be done. I knew enough to know what I think I wanted. But, on one hand, I was asking for more than I needed. And, on the other hand, I had no idea what I already had. The grounding issue turned out to be minor. But Electrician One didn't do the simplest test to verify that I knew what I thought I knew.

Electrician One made this all about money. And left a potential $7,000 on the table.

Electricians Two were far more professional in every way. They worked from assumptions of success.

Successful Assumption One: We're going to do the job right. There is a right way to do this. It's in the client's best interest to do it the right way. Avoid the discussion of "Can we do it cheaper?" until the client brings it up.

Successful Assumption Two: Know what you know. Unless your client is in your business, verify that what they tell you is accurate. It's not that the client's lying, but they simply don't know. (And even if they're in your business, it's still good to verify.)

Successful Assumption Three: Deliver your pricing very matter-of-factly and without apologies. This company actually had a very good technique: They pre-printed several common tasks and listed a high/low range for each. Then they quoted the low end of that range.

Electricians Two also added an overall air of professionalism in how they presented themselves and their work. There was no talk about cutting corners. They didn't say so, but I found myself comparing their professionalism to their competition.

I did get a third quote around $4,500, but decided to go with the more professional, higher-end contractor. In part, it's because their overall approach is very much in line with mine. They can be passed over in favor of other contractors and still be okay. Why? They can get rejected for nine jobs at $800 each and still come out ahead with one job at $8,300.

They work from a mentality of abundance and not a mentality of scarcity.

"Your" Way

So what's the "Your Company Way" that defines your branding? What guiding principles do you use for employee onboarding, sales, service delivery, billing, and every other thing in your business?

In the next chapter we'll talk about this with a focus on documentation. You might be tempted to say, "We have no SOPs," or "We don't have a consistent way of doing things." But that's rarely true. You do invoicing: How do you do it? You hire people: How do you go about it? You deliver services: How do you do it?

As you go through this book, I encourage you to start collecting ideas that reflect *your way* of doing things. Perhaps keep a folder or a document on your laptop or tablet. Start with my Absolutely Unbreakable Rules and work from there. Cross out what doesn't apply, edit some, add others. Make it your own.

And it's okay if some of these are aspirational. That is, you want them to be your rules even though you don't follow them today.

My Absolutely Unbreakable Rules are included in the downloads that accompany this book. Go to www.absolutelyunbreakablerules.com to register your book. I have them in both PDF and Word docx formats.

5. Documentation and the E-Myth

Perhaps the luckiest thing that happened to me in 1995 is that I read *The E-Myth Revisited* by Michael Gerber for the first time. (I have re-read it many times since then.)

A friend heard that I was going to quit my job and go into business for myself as a contractor. He recommended the book. It was very consistent with how I had managed departments and corporate offices in my job, so it made perfect sense to me. But it also starts out with a story about a one-person company and tells the tale of how you set up that company for a successful future.

Gerber looks at why companies fail and, more importantly, why some companies do not fail. Most (like 80%) small businesses do not last five years. And of those who survive, most don't make it another five years. So, if you've been in business for five or ten or fifteen years, you must be doing something right.

Overwhelmingly, one key to success is documenting your processes. Perhaps the most important element in my success, with every business I have built or managed, is my insistence on documentation. My writing career has been dominated by helping people document their processes. Some related books include:

- *The Network Documentation Workbook*
- *Managed Services in a Month*
- *Cloud Services in a Month*
- *The Network Migration Workbook* (with Manuel Palachuk)
- *The Managed Services Operations Manual*—four volume set
- *Project Management in Small Business* (with Dana Goulston)

All of these are filled with forms, processes, and procedures.

I am writing this chapter on a plane, which is a common occurrence for me. One time, I was flying home and sitting next to a friend of mine. I was writing a chapter for *The Managed Services Operations Manual* on how to use Velcro.

She looked at me as if I was from Mars. "Your readers don't know how to use Velcro?"

Well, I suppose everyone can figure it out. But to me, there's a right way and a wrong way.

Little things like this truly separate the pros from the newbies. Every profession has "little things" that you learn over time from trial and error—or working with a pro. Clients may never notice the little things. But they will benefit from the little things. And sometimes, as with Velcro, they *will* notice if you do it wrong.

Velcro has two components—one is scratchy and one is soft. The single most important rule of using Velcro to mount equipment is that you ALWAYS put the soft side on the bottom of the equipment. I go into more detail in the SOP, but the primary reason is that if the equipment is ever placed on a wooden desk or other "nice" surface, it won't scratch it up.

Also, from time to time, you will need to stack some equipment. When you do that, you will always need to have one side of the Velcro on the top and another side on the bottom. Whichever side is on top must always be on top. And whichever side is on the bottom must always be on the bottom. That way, anything can be stacked on anything and you don't have to think about it.

Similarly, if you are mounting equipment on a shelf of a wall, the same side must always be on the shelf of the wall. And thus every piece of equipment can easily be moved to any shelf or any wall— because it's consistent.

The only reason I point this out here is to make the point: *Everything* needs to be documented—no matter how small it is! If you have *Your Company Way* of doing something, that needs to be documented.

And it gets better!

You can never document one hundred percent of everything, but you can get close. The world changes too much to ever maintain one hundred percent, even if you could reach it. If you can document eighty or ninety percent, then the rest can often take care of itself.

If your employees understand and follow your SOPs, they will understand a bigger picture that represents your company. So, when they are faced with a new, undocumented task, they will probably do what you would have done. They know how you operate, how you approach service delivery, how to talk to clients about it, etc.

So when they have to make something up on the fly, the chances are very good that they will make the right decisions.

Processes Are Branding.
Branding Is Everything You Do.

I have done a lot of work with franchises. There are good franchises and bad franchises. The best franchises have the most detailed handbooks.

One of my favorite examples is Subway sandwich shops. How did Subway get to be the largest food franchise in the world—run by a bunch of seventeen- and eighteen-year-olds? Standard Operating Procedures.

Let me finish this chapter with another great book by Michael Gerber: *E-Myth Mastery*. In this book, Gerber spells out the mindset that will help you build a truly great organization. The key element is simple but profound: Build a business that is bigger than you are.

What does that mean? It means that your business won't die just because you do. It means your business will hum right along when you go on vacation for two weeks, or two months. It means that your processes and procedures are so well-defined that any single person in your company can be replaced and the organization will still be successful.

And brings us right back to where we started: Documentation.

A great organization documents what they will do and what they have done. They document how things are done, and why things are done that way.

Think about the evolution of a business. Here are some stages to consider.

1) Nothing is documented. Therefore, things are not very standardized. Clients and employees do not expect consistency. The owner makes all the decisions.

2) Some things are documented. Some things are standardized. Clients and employees expect some consistency. The owner makes almost all the decisions.

3) Most things are documented. Most things are standardized. Clients and employees expect consistency. The owner makes sure the process is followed.

4) Everything is documented. Everything is standardized. Clients and employees rely on consistency. The owner checks in with the managers who make sure the processes are followed.

I hope you see why I insist that "branding" is everything you do. It's not just that you greet people in a friendly way, but that both customers and employees understand that there's a certain *way* you do business.

The Way cannot be locked inside your head. The Way permeates every aspect of your business. It can be known. It can be shared. It creates your culture. It is your brand.

6. The Way You Do Anything . . .

> "The way you do anything is the way you do everything."
> — Tom Waits

I love this quote—even if it's not always true. It goes hand in hand with "You can't judge a book by its cover." Everyone *does* judge a book by its cover: That's how we decide which books to buy.

And by default, your clients and prospects will believe that the way you do anything is the way you do everything. If your sales process shows you to be inaccurate or difficult to communicate with, they will believe that that's how you are in other things.

That's why, in Chapter 2, I introduced the emphasis on process (You can't control people, but you can control your processes). When you think about "your way" and your SOPs, it's important to note that everything you do in your company falls into one of two categories:

1) Behaviors you created with intention
2) Behaviors that emerged on their own

It's extremely important that more of your behaviors fall into the first category. This includes technical processes as well as culture and the softer (human) side of your business. There are three periods during which you need to be attentive to that long list of "everything" you do: Before the sale, your first job for the client, and your ongoing relationship.

Before the Sale

Whether you realize it or not, your sales process tells a story about how you will be to work with. Do you have pre-printed forms? Do you give a written estimate? Are you easy to get ahold of by phone or email?

I intentionally mention that we have a process for everything when I'm in a sales cycle. I always use the phrase "We like to see . . ." to describe what we would do with the prospect's network. We like to see a business class firewall. We like to see a monthly test of the backup. And so forth.

This casually lets the client know that we have a process. And it subtly says that we expect them to follow it.

Whether you like it or not, you will be judged very broadly based on your sales process.

The First Job

In the Managed Services Operations Manual, I have a whole chapter on the first job. Basically, this is the most important job you do for the client. It sets the tone for everything that will follow.

This will be the first time you show up for a work order. How do you show up? What do you wear? How do you greet the client? How do you explain what you'll be doing? How do you manage the money and the paperwork?

If you're working from a quote, it's very important that you charge what you said you would charge. Avoid a change order at all costs, if you can.

If you haven't thought about it, you should. What do you normally do on a first job? How does it go? How do you control as much of the process as you can?

It's particularly important that you don't let the first job morph into a big, messy, catch-all job. Do exactly what you agreed to and make it as successful as possible. Then create a service ticket for each additional item the client wants to add to the list. You don't need to say no, but you do need to say, "Not now." If you allow scope creep on the first job, you can expect it on many jobs after this.

I know some of you are thinking that this is "bad" service because I'm not running around trying to get ten hours' worth of work into a two-hour visit. But there's a good reason for this policy: You need to establish a pattern of support that is sustainably profitable.

The Ongoing Relationship

This is where the real payoff is. You need to practice consistency in all things. This is very important as you grow your company. When you are a small shop (five or fewer), every client gets to know every technician. As you grow, that becomes harder to do.

One time I was talking to a former client and we were discussing the various technicians we experienced over the 20 years they were my client. She mentioned one guy who really stood out—for the wrong reasons. Apparently, when he started, people in her company weren't sure they liked him or his personality.

"But," she said, "we know you and we know the kinds of people you hire. And we had faith that he would do a good job." And, over time, he won them over. More importantly, the consistency of our performance over time won them over.

In all these things, you need to steer the ship. Wherever you are right now, you need to make sure that you are attentive to the "everything" and move it in the right direction. If a process is well-defined and exactly what you want going forward, make sure it's documented and everyone is trained on it.

If a process is poorly defined, or your company doesn't consistently do it the way you want, then you need to define how it should be, and train everybody up on that. Little by little, all processes will improve over time. Documentation and training are your best tools.

I have said on many occasions that employees and clients are like dogs: They will do whatever you train them to do. This includes training by not training. If you train employees to do whatever they want at the client's office, that's what they'll do. If you train clients that they can call you in the evening, they will.

I highly encourage you to have a formal documentation process. Keep your documentation in a place where everyone can get to it. Train employees to look for a written process first and to follow it. Train them to update the process if necessary. The last item on every checklist should be to update the checklist.

I guess the way you document anything is the way you document everything.

☺

Next, let's start looking at those Absolutely Unbreakable Rules!

Section III
General Rules for Successful Service Delivery

7. Prioritize Everything

8. Do Not be Interrupt-Driven

9. Slow Down, Get More Done

10. Know What You Know

11. The Competition Is Irrelevant

12. We Only Work with People We Like

7. Prioritize Everything

> Note: Several chapters start with a big **thumbs up**. That's not on every chapter, but I promise you, when you see this at the top of a chapter: If you just do this one thing, it will pay for the cost of this book a thousand times over!
>
> And I promise, there isn't a thumbs up in every chapter.

Rule number one is: **Prioritize Everything**.

You should prioritize everything in both your personal life and in your business. This is why I love having a CRM (customer relationship management) or PSA (professional services automation) tool, or some other tool to track tasks. A PSA allows me to create a ticket for absolutely everything that needs to be done, inside the company and with clients.

Once you prioritize everything, a lot of problems go away.

Many people say, "Well, how do I manage time? I've got all of my technicians stacked up and there's always too much to do." Well, one way to do it is to stop paying attention to time. Don't schedule anything unless you have to and always let employees work from the highest to lowest priority. Let me repeat that:

> Don't schedule anything unless you have to.
> Always let employees work from the
> highest to lowest priority.

For example, let's look at high priority tickets. Once an employee identifies the highest priority tickets, he should work from the oldest ticket to the newest. So: **highest to lowest, oldest to newest**. That formula allows employees to assign to themselves the highest-priority task that they can accomplish and then things begin to move really fast.

When everyone in your company is working on the highest-priority task that they can, your business can get an amazing amount of work done!

You can create any kind of priority system you want, but the simpler the better. I'm a huge fan of a very simple system:

Priority One =	Emergency
Priority Two =	High
Priority Three =	Medium
Priority Four =	Low

A few notes. First, no human being can set a P1. Emergencies set themselves. That means even the owner or the operations manager cannot "declare" a P1 (emergency). A true emergency affects the entire company. It is either a company-wide outage or a smaller outage that causes the company to be losing money.

Second, humans can set high, medium, and low priorities. The default should be medium priority. That means you can't let everyone make everything high priority. At the same time, you need to develop processes so that low priority tickets get attention. Obviously, true emergencies get attention immediately. They are, after all, true emergencies.

When it comes to high priority tasks and tickets, you need to ask the question, "How urgent is this?" This allows you to tease out whether something is truly high priority. For example, fixing the printer before payroll has to be printed is extremely important. But if that's two weeks away, it doesn't have to be fixed immediately before anything else can move forward.

Once you start being rational with priorities, your clients will as well. It might take quite a while to make the transition, but eventually your priorities will reflect the true importance of everything that needs to be done in your company. Emergencies will be few and far between. There will be a manageable handful of high priority tasks. Most things on your to-do list will be medium priority. And all low priority tasks will be scheduled and taken care of.

I know this sounds impossible to some of you. But you really need to believe me: It's shockingly easy once you start believing in *the system*. The system is true. It's proven in millions of businesses over the years. It's very easy. But it takes time and commitment. Commit to it, and it will become true.

Note: Once you start prioritizing, you'll realize that low priority items need special attention. Isn't that ironic? Clients will put attention on low priority items because they worry that you'll ignore them. And you will start developing rules to make sure that low-priority items get some attention.

Did you notice that I said that low priority stuff needs to get scheduled? Overall, you want to avoid scheduling unless you have to. But you also need strategies to make sure the low priority items get done eventually. One method is to occasionally look at all the things that need to be done for one client and try to knock them all out at once. Thus, low priority items are tackled.

Another option is to actually assign someone to only work on low priority items. Yet another is to work on low priority items whenever you happen to send someone on site at the client's office.

As you can see, there are many ways to move things forward.

I'm sure you've seen the diagram from the book *The Power of Focus* by Jack Canfield, Leslie Hewitt, and Mark Victor Hansen. The diagram divides four cells into Urgent/Not Urgent and Important/ Not Important. Something like this:

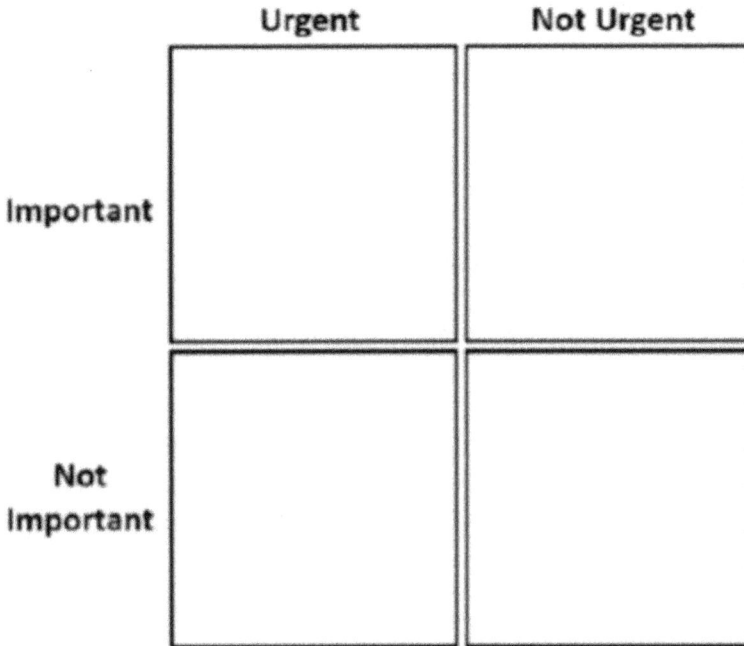

	Urgent	Not Urgent
Important		
Not Important		

We spend a lot of time in the urgent but not important category. You should spend none of your time in the unimportant categories, even if it's urgent. And "urgent" often simply means that somebody came into your office or knocked on your door. Now they've interrupted your flow and you're working on their stuff instead of your stuff, and it might not be the single most important thing you need to be doing right then.

In fact, it's almost certainly *not* the most important thing you need to be doing.

Many people have great difficulty with priorities because they have a sense that "everything" is high priority. Or even the highest priority. That simply can't be. For the most part, the sense that everything is high priority is a great indicator that you are working in the "urgent" quadrants and not the "important" quadrants.

Balancing Priorities - Easier Said Than Done

Let's assume that you want to start working based on priorities. Great! How do you get started? Here are a few tips.

There are two primary components of this: The logjam, and competing priorities. The logjam happens when there are too many "high" priority items are on your list. This might be because you're new to prioritizing and don't know how to actually figure out what's first and what's second. Or it can happen during a "crunch" period when lots of things get dumped in your lap at once.

Competing priorities are much more common after you've been prioritizing awhile. Some things naturally fall into categories of high, medium, and low. And the place where we see the conflict is almost always in the high priority category.

Strangely enough, the best long-term strategy for dealing with priorities is practice. And, yes, I understand that doesn't help today, in this minute, in this crunch. But over time, you get better at things you do more often. So, the practice of prioritizing makes you better at prioritizing. As with so many things, it's easiest to deal with before the big crunch comes.

Here are a few tips for working through your big list of high priority items.

1. Step back and look at even higher-level values. For example, getting to your kid's playoff game versus getting out a big quote for a client. The higher-level values are family vs. money. I use this example because it's one of the most common - and hardest to deal with. It also gets to the real hard part of choosing between priorities. In the abstract, you might choose family. But you can't choose family every time or there won't be any money! And, of course, you

can't choose money every time or there won't be a family to come home to. And that leads to #2.

2. Who won last time? Sometimes, you have constant priority battles that recur all the time. When you think in terms of an ongoing, never-ending series of choices, then stepping back allows you to look at a different level of balance. If two competing high priority values are always coming up against one another, how do you choose?

One long-term option is to work on a balance that is comfortable - even if you'd rather not admit it. Perhaps you'll want to say that family will win about 70% of the time and money will win 30%. If money has to win some of the time, at least you're being realistic about it.

3. Time Slice. Many high-priority items are basically non-stop. Whether it's the laundry at home or invoicing at work, there are some chores that never end. Allocate time to each, even if you never get everything done. There are times when "zero in-box" or a clean desk are simply not realistic options.

Once you admit that more email will come in, and more invoicing always has to go out, these become ongoing tasks. Allocate an hour to each; make as much progress as you can; move on to something else.

4. Pick the priority that can be finished fastest. Sometimes you can see that three or four hours of focused effort will get a big item off your list. Work on that one big item until it's complete . . . or as complete as you can make it at this time. Once you take care of the "big rocks," you relieve a lot of pressure from your overall system.

5. Reach a milestone and pass the task to someone else. Another favorite of mine: Get to a milestone. Since I work with a lot of other people, I can make a lot of progress by moving a project to a specific point and then passing it along to someone else. For example, when

I write, I sometimes pass chapters to my layout and proof-reading folks as I finish each chapter.

There might be changes down the road, but the overall project is moved forward. Very often, I can get a major piece of something done even if I can't get the whole thing done. Then I feel better about moving to the next high priority item and moving that forward.

6. Get Help! And all of the items above work better if you have help. In the 21st century, "getting help" no longer means hiring someone full time. You can hire someone part time. Or hire someone over the Internet - in another city or even another country. I have outsourced resources for graphics, administrative work, bookkeeping, layout, proof-reading, marketing, language translation, audio production, and more. The best part about this kind of modern outsourcing is that I don't have to manage people. I manage jobs.

The biggest message of all: **Don't pretend this will stop!**

Don't pretend that you will break through the current backlog and everything will be wonderful. That day will never come. Work IS like the laundry. As soon as you think it's done, another pair of socks gets thrown in the basket. As soon as today's priorities are dealt with, another set appears out of nowhere.

And that's the way it should be. A never-ending series of tasks and priorities is what keeps you busy - and in business. Don't wish for it to go away. Manage it.

Things Undone

Here's a little reality check for you. In the end, the very lowest priority tasks will probably never get done.

I know that's startling.

The lowest priority tasks will never get done. And, to be honest, at some point you will die with work undone. You will. I don't want to be morbid, but it's true.

When I say this in live presentations, someone always asks if this is the motivational part of the presentation. But we all know that people who are irreplaceable leave or die every day. Steve Jobs died. Apple is more successful today, and more profitable than they've ever been. Bill Gates left Microsoft (he didn't die), and they're more profitable today than they've ever been.

It's just a fact: You will have lots of things that are low priority that you will never get to. That's not a bad thing, and you're not an evil person for accepting that that's the truth. One reason that many people suck at goal-setting is that they are unwilling to assign any tasks to the lowest priority or to admit that items in the lowest priority category will never get done.

It's okay to have zero guilt about the fact that the lowest priority things in your life will never get done.

The important question is: How do you make sure that the most important things DO get done? Luckily, that's easy: Work on the highest priority things first.

Be aware of the downside to this: It will piss off people who think that they should be able to interrupt you all the time. A handful actually think they have that right. Most people simply think it's rude for you to ignore them. But if you're working on the single most important thing you have to do, then you should and must ignore them!

If you've followed me for long, you know that I never answer my phone. Well, 99% of the time. Some people get really angry about this. They call. They even leave voicemails (I stopped checking voicemail). They text and ask me to answer my phone!

Eventually, they either give up or email me and schedule a time to connect by phone. Miraculously, that works. You see, random phone calls are never, ever the single most important thing I have to pay attention to in my life or my business.

Here's a very interesting irony about this rule: The single most important person in my life is, and has been for almost thirty years, my daughter. And guess what? I never answer the phone when she calls unless I happen to have it in my hand and be looking at the screen when she calls. And sometimes even then I don't answer it. The irony is, she doesn't care. It doesn't bother her the least little bit. She knows she's important to me, and that I will communicate with her. Whenever she needs me, I'm there. So she's surprised when I *do* answer the phone.

And she's the same way. If I call her, I fully expect to leave a message. I never expect her to answer the phone. She's got a job and a life. And she's probably in the middle of something when I call. (She also turns off her ringer or turns off her phone altogether, just like her old man.)

Telephone etiquette aside, people also want to interrupt you at meetings, in your office, or just walking down the hallway. Idle chit-chat is one thing. But if you are doing something important, then you should not allow interruptions. And that will irritate people.

Very often, I have to remind my employees that I *am* ignoring them, but they should not be offended. I want them to work from highest to lowest priority, and I do the same. That means that I often have something higher priority than whatever they're emailing about.

None of them has nothing to do, so they can simply move to the next priority on their list until I get back to them. And I have strategies in place to catch up with everyone and address all the questions. It takes work, and a dedication to the priority process. But in the long run, it is far more efficient than working on the most recent thing that interrupted you just because it's the most recent thing that interrupted you!

8. Do Not be Interrupt-Driven

This rule obviously follows from the first one. I'm a huge fan of silencing my phone and having it off at all times. With rare exceptions, for example when I'm expecting a call, my phone is off, and it's usually in another room.

I always ask people: Let's say that your phone rings right now. What's the probability that it is the single most important thing that you need to be doing in your business right now? Probably zero, if not very close to zero. **So stop answering your phone**. Really.

About 2005, I adopted a rule that no one in my companies is allowed to answer the phone. We call people back. Many people ask how this is possible in the world of business.

Consider this experience (I know this has happened to you): You're in a meeting or a training and your phone is on silent. A client calls. An hour later you call them back and they say, "Oh yeah, I'm really glad you called. I need this and this and this."

That's it. Thanks for returning my call.

They don't know that you were offline. They don't know that you were ignoring them. They just know that you called them back in a reasonable amount of time and everything's okay.

I challenge you to try this. Tomorrow, get up, silence your phone, never answer it, and *only call people back*. No one will notice. Really. Now, you need to check your phone at least every two hours. And almost all the messages will be spam. And there won't be any emergencies.

The reason that I adopted this policy is because of a client experience. I was down in the Sacramento Delta where cell service was sketchy at the time. I was putting up a piece of equipment on a shelf. I was on top of a ladder when my cell phone rang.

I climbed down the ladder, but by then it had gone to voicemail. So, I climbed back up the ladder and the phone rang again. I climbed back down and tried to answer it, but the call dropped. At this point I decide to see what's going on, so I used the client's landline to check my voicemail. It was a client, screaming, "Where are you? I need you right now! When I call, I need you to answer me right away!" Just yelling and screaming, for three messages.

I called her back from the landline and I said, "Hey, I want to talk about expectations."

And she says, "I don't want to talk about that."

I said, "No, we need to talk about that. We need to talk about what's a reasonable response."

She said, "A reasonable response is you answer the phone every single time I call on the first ring."

I said, "No, that is not a reasonable response. It is now seven minutes since your first phone call and I have called you back after listening to you scream at me on three different messages. This is not reasonable. Let's talk about what is reasonable."

But she was adamant: She must have her phone call answered on the first ring.

Anyway, I calmed her down and solved her (completely non-urgent) problem. Then I went and had a talk with her boss. He said that even though we had worked together for almost ten years, he stood behind his employee. And I said, "Okay. I will help you find another IT consultant, because this expectation is unreasonable, and we will not do business with you."

And then I went back to my office and I told people that they are no longer allowed to answer their phones, period. We call people back. It puts us in charge of the communications and it allows us to stay focused on the single most important thing we should be doing at that given moment.

And, if you think about it, somebody right now wants to raise their hand and ask the ultimate question I get in every presentation for the last 15 years: "What happens if the server goes out at midnight?" Look, bad things happen. But *you cannot build your business around the exception to the rule.* Don't build your life around the exception to the rule. Emergencies are, by definition, rare.

How many of the phone calls in your life have been true over-the-top emergencies? Almost none, and for many people reading this book, actually none. So, don't build your life as if you have to be interrupted by the phone.

The second worst interrupter is Microsoft Outlook. When I get a new Outlook client, it probably takes me fifteen or twenty minutes to make that thing shut up. I have a Kindle and an iPad, and I have to silence all the notifications on those as well.

Outlook wants to interrupt you all the time, all day long. So do the web sites you subscribe to, the social media outlets, the apps, etc. Almost every site you visit on the Internet has a popup that asks if they can send you notifications.

NO! The answer is no. No interruptions. Period.

The Interruption Diet

Here's a great exercise for making interruptions visible to you. Create an "Interruption Diet" like this:

Interruption	Time Start / Stop	Importance	Notes
Example: **Phone Call**	*8:45 am— 8:50 am*	*Not!*	*Sales call. Grrr.*

Create a whole sheet like this for each day of the week. Or just use lined note paper. This is much like a food diet for keeping track of what you ate today, but The Interruption Diet is literally just a sheet so you can write down what time something interrupted you (or attempted to).

Give some detail. For example, that the phone call was from a salesperson. Next, rate how important it was. And how long the interruption lasted.

Keep track of all interruptions for the next week. For example:

- When somebody knocks on your door
- When someone wants to come into your office
- When you're doing something and somebody wants your attention immediately
- When the phone rings

Whatever the interruption, write it down. This will only take a second. Do this for one business day and what you'll see is that you have far more interruptions than you thought you had and they're far less important. At the end of a week, you'll see how much potential interruption you have.

The fact that somebody's at your door does not mean that you have to answer it. The fact somebody calls you on the phone does not mean that you have to answer it. You should take control of your life, and if those priorities matter, then the way to put them in place is to not let yourself be driven by other people.

I have a couple of relevant phrases that I love to repeat.

1. Clients are like dogs. They will do exactly what you have trained them to do.
2. Employees are like dogs. They will do exactly what you've trained them to do.

If you let your clients call you anytime, anywhere, they expect that to be the case. If you take control of the communications and call them back in a reasonable amount of time, they will have a much higher impression of your responsiveness than you ever imagined.

Even with my rules, I constantly have people say things like, "Thanks for getting back to me so quickly." Or, "I didn't expect such a quick reply." You have to respond in a reasonable amount of time. But that does not mean instantly.

Somebody was making a little video about my company several years ago and a client who had been with me for more than ten years said on video, "Karl's so amazingly responsive and we call him any time of the day or night and he's just always there for us." Well, that's not true. As far as I know, he's never called me after six p.m. in ten years, but if he did, I didn't answer the phone. Still, it is his impression that we are super-responsive, because we do get back to people.

One day I was in the local Target store. Right up front they have a few shelves full of miscellaneous junk for one or two dollars each. Sometimes they have little orange emergency cones, four for a dollar. They look like roadside emergency cones, but they're about the size of a coffee mug.

One day I saw these emergency cones and thought, "Oh, this is perfect!" And I bought all that they had and gave them to my employees. Now, every employee has two orange emergency cones.

If you watch my videos on YouTube, you sometimes see them in the background (www.youtube.com/smallbizthoughts).

If an employee puts out one cone, it means they are very busy. If they put out two cones, they are not to be interrupted for any reason. So, for example, my administrative assistant can put out two cones and I will not interrupt her no matter what, unless the building's on fire. This is a process you can put in place so that you acknowledge the priorities of your employees, and that if they are in fact working on the single most important thing that they can do for your company. Let them finish their job.

We have massive amounts of research about interruptions. If you get interrupted, it can take you five to twenty minutes to get back on track. Imagine being interrupted. Look at the interruption diet. You might add another column there for how long it took you to get back on track with what you were doing. It can be quite significant.

Final Note on Phones

I know we have trained ourselves (since forever) that we have to answer the phone. It's just not true.

I am often asked about a reasonable response time. You won't believe it, but the next day is usually fine. In reality, I now check my phone once per day. But I let employees check their phones every two hours. That's three or four times per day.

If you respond within fifteen to thirty minutes, I don't think there are any reasonable people who will expect a faster response. Your clients know that you run a service business and you are often out delivering service.

The first time I was running an IT department (back when I had a real job), we had somebody working on our larger computers. This guy used to always take calls from other clients while he was working at our office. He'd go out in the hallway and walk back and forth. All I could think of was the fact that he was spending our money and somebody else's money at the same time. I didn't like that.

This was about 1993. I told him, "If you're going to take phone calls, I want to make damn sure you are off my clock." And he said, "Well, sometimes stuff comes up and blah, blah."

I said I don't care. "I know stuff comes up. Get off my clock if you're going to go take that call."

Your clients don't want you to treat them like this. Given the trade-off between taking calls for another client while at their office, they would rather have all of your attention in a reasonable amount of time. For most of you, if you respond within an hour, your clients probably won't even notice the difference.

Final story. One time we moved from one office to another. My marketing manager, Monica, put her phone on the floor next to her desk. I said, "What is your phone doing on the floor?"

And she said, "Oh. I'm not going to answer it. And you're not going to answer it. So why should it take up space on my desk?"

And that's actually current. Shortly after that, we moved to just having voicemail and no phones.

How Do You Minimize Interruptions?

If interruptions are coming from an outsider, including clients, it is easy to set up rules to deal with this. But insiders (your employees) are a different story. You can't have rules that keep them from doing their job successfully. So you need to look at the causes of interruption.

The three largest causes of interruption from employees are knowledge, training, and authority.

Lack of knowledge is different from lack of training. Lack of knowledge could be as simple as knowing the alarm code to get into a client's office. This lack of knowledge is addressed through proper documentation.

Look at your interruption diet. If you glossed over it because you didn't think you needed to do the exercise, maybe it's time to actually do it. Anyway, look at your interruptions from employees. How many of them were about knowledge generally? Where do we keep the xxx? What's the logon for that? Where are the licenses kept? And so forth.

Most of the time, failure to pass knowledge to employees happens because the boss/owner feels that they're too busy to document. Fine: Make the employees document! Every time they ask for information, make them document where it is or should be found. Whether you take the time or your employees take the time, someone has to document your processes. I love having everyone involved. I also love empowering everyone to improve the process every time they use it. This leads to continuous incremental improvement. We'll come back to that topic.

Lack of training means that the main reason an employee needs to interrupt you is that they don't have the skillset to get something done. This might mean that they don't know your internal process or that they do not master a certain skill or technology. Both are obviously fixable.

One of the things you probably never thought about when you started your business is that you need to train your employees (and yourself)—forever! Training people on internal processes goes a long way to eliminate the lack of knowledge we just talked about. And training them on techniques and tools keeps your business moving ahead with the latest skills in your industry.

Again, look at your interruption diet results. How many of your interruptions are related to employees who do not know how to perform a skill or service that's important to their job? And how will you fix that?

I'm a huge fan of training in all forms. That means having employees train each other, take classes, read books, watch videos, take exams, get certified, and whatever else they can do. Improving your employees' skills improves your business!

There's an old humorous story about the business owner who complains: What if I spend all this money training people and then they leave? Well, what happens if you don't train them and they stay?

It is obviously in your best interest to train your employees and to encourage their self-study. The reality is that they will probably not work for you for the rest of their lives. Taking actions to build up their skills and talents will help them advance their career. In the short term, you get a better employee—and one who is committed to you because you have invested in them. In the end, they will probably stay longer if they see that you are helping them reach up the ladder of success.

The final reason that employees interrupt the owner or boss is that they **lack the authority** to act on their own. This is actually one of the most critical measures of a successful business.

Why doesn't your team have the ability to execute without you? In some cases, this is part of the division of job duties. For example, a task might require manager approval. Consider how useful or necessary that rule is.

Much more commonly, employees cannot perform tasks simply because the real authority still remains with the owner or manager. This is a weakness in the owner or manager. It might be a desire to retain power, or a reluctance to believe that the team can actually do the job. Again, that goes back to training.

The worst thing you can do when it comes to delegation is to delegate in name only and retain the actual authority. This leads to making you the chokepoint for everything in your company. True delegation includes the delegation of authority to actually make decisions.

You cannot delegate in name only. When employees feel that they cannot make the smallest decision simply because it will probably be overridden by the boss—for no good reason—they tend to give up making any decision. In other words, bad delegation leads to an even worse chokepoint.

And, of course, it means that you get interrupted all day long. Thus, you've become the biggest chokepoint in the office, and even you can't get any work done.

Obviously, this is more than simply a pet peeve for me. Having worked with thousands of businesses over the years, I believe constant interruption may be the biggest sign of a broken business. Luckily, it can all be solved with a series of intentional processes that you put in place.

Fix it!

9. Slow Down, Get More Done

This is so central to my life and my business that I had a poster made for my wall that says, "Slow down, get more done." There are so many levels to this advice.

The simplest one is that sometimes you are so intent and frustrated in your work that you cannot make progress. For example, if you're working on something intently, your head's down, and you're pounding against the computer. You are trying and trying and trying, but you just cannot solve the problem. Then, you take a break, splash some water on your face, walk around the block, you sit down, and suddenly you solve the problem right away.

This is because you've let your brain relax, and you've taken a little timeout.

Here's another example. Let's say one of your customers has an emergency. Should you immediately jump in the car and drive over there? Probably not. It is usually better to take stock of what your resources are. Who else has equipment like that? Who else can work on this problem? Which is the best technician? How far away are they? What kind of warranty coverage does the client have?

Slow down, get more done.

You've heard your entire life that you should think before you speak. We need to take a breath before we act. If you've ever had kids, you know the deal. Many, many problems are solved by taking a deep breath before you start talking or moving.

A couple years ago, I was talking to an Uber driver. She said the best lesson her father ever taught her about driving is to pause **one**

second when the light turns green. Just sit for one second before you go. She said it has saved her from more than one accident over the years. Ever since I heard that advice, I do the same thing.

One of my favorite old humorous work complaints is: "We never have time to do it right, but we always have time to do it over." Slow down, get more done.

Documentation

This rule also applies to documentation. So many business owners tell me that they don't have time to create documentation. I say that's total B.S.

Documenting your processes is absolutely guaranteed to make you more money in the long run for several reasons. First, it allows you to train people very quickly. It forces you to think through your process and organize it. Second, it creates standardization through your organization and over time. "Standard" operating procedures always save money!

Third, it allows you to quickly expand your workforce as needed. You can hire competent people, hand them your process, and know that they will be able to execute the procedure exactly as you would. The example I use in technology is that any good computer consultant can set up a laptop machine. But if I give them my checklist, any of them can set it up exactly as I would.

SOPs (standard operating procedures) help you to build your brand. This is the way you do it.

Less successful service companies provide inconsistent service. This is due in large part to a lack of SOPs. They hire technicians (roofers, plumbers, attorneys, etc.) and then let them figure it out for themselves. That gets a job done, but gets it done inconsistently across employees. And it doesn't help you build your brand. "Let everyone do it however they want" is *not* a brand!

Documenting *your* process takes a little time, but a lot less than most people think. It always helps build your brand.

Training

Just like documentation, training "costs" you time, but pays for itself in the long run. With documentation, we're thinking in terms of defining something. It might be a configuration or a process. With training, the focus is on education. That education might rely on the documentation, but training is beyond documentation.

Perhaps the most obvious place where training will help you to *slow down and get more done* is when an owner or manager is learning to delegate authority. Don't stop reading just because you've been a manager for several years! I can't tell you how many owners and managers I've worked with who are very ineffective at delegating— even after ten years of doing it!

When you are handing work to someone else, it will always be faster to just do it yourself. You have to consciously choose to train someone to do the job. They will be slower than you. They may not do as well as you. But you have to have faith that they will learn their job—and be better than you eventually!

And, of course, the benefits of training others multiply. The people you train will eventually train others. At each level of growth, your company is capable of doing more and more work because you have slowed down just enough to increase your capacity again and again.

Planning, Strategy, and Quiet Time

Finally, the most productive way to apply this rule is simply to sit in a chair and think about your business. You can read a hundred books on business success and find that ninety of them will include this advice: Take time to think about your business.

That might mean taking quiet time every morning to set your

intentions for the day, or planning out the three things you hope to accomplish. It might mean strategy sessions with other people. It might mean creating a "mastermind group" you can participate in. However you let planning and strategy time manifest themselves in your business, you must do something. There is lots of advice along these lines that sounds like a bunch of clichés—but that doesn't mean the advice is bad.

- Before you start climbing the ladder of success, make sure it's leaning against the right wall.
- If you don't know where you're going, any road will get you there.

My favorite is a book title by Sylvia Boorstein:

- *Don't Just Do Something, Sit There.*

Time spent thinking about your business is never wasted. Even if you decide not to make any changes, you will have affirmed your current course. But, more often than not, you will spend the time improving your business, whether that's developing new marketing programs, deciding which products to sell, or restructuring your org chart. It's all good work.

Too many entrepreneurs fall into the false belief that the only productive activity is something that looks productive to others. So, they dig into computer-work or fidgety labor rather than sitting in a chair with a tablet of paper and just thinking about tomorrow, next week, next month, and next year.

They confuse busy-ness with business. It's as if you get extra points for looking busy, even if you're wasting time.

There is a thing called "Type A Behavior" that is known to kill people. It is highly correlated with heart disease, high blood pressure, and all kinds of stress-related health issues. And guess what? The people most likely to exhibit Type A Behavior are entrepreneurs! What does it look like?

Type A Behavior includes things like working long hours, well past the time when you have stopped being productive. It includes choosing caffeine over exercise or restful sleep. It is typified by believing that no one will do the job as good as you, so you end up working more and more.

That's an amazing irony, isn't it? As a business grows and hires more people, the owner is very likely to put in more hours and more hours, half-delegating, and ultimately being responsible for more and more.

Until his heart explodes.

No joke.

The real irony is that you will be more productive, your company will be more productive, you will make more money in the long run, and you will enjoy a higher quality of life when you learn to let other people do the jobs you hired them to do.

It's okay to go home. It's okay to recharge your batteries. It's okay to relax and enjoy your success.

Again, I know it sounds cliché, but there's truth in the observation that some people work so hard that they forget to develop a real family life or hobbies. And then they retire, have no idea what to do with themselves, and die before their time. It happens all the time. I have known more than one person who was afraid to retire because they had no hobbies—and didn't know whether they could spend all day, every day, doing "nothing" for the rest of their lives.

Slow down, get more done.

Build your business and your life with intention. Create a beautiful balance that you can enjoy forever. And, oddly enough, you'll discover that it's much easier to give it up if your business is so successful that it works well without you.

And who knows? You may never need to give it up if your business is a delightfully balanced and integral part of your life.

In case you haven't read it yet, I recommend you take a look at my book *Relax Focus Succeed: Balance Your Personal and Professional Lives and Be More Successful in Both.*

Consider all the places where your business can benefit from slowing down just a little and getting more done in the long run. Once you start learning to apply this, you'll see opportunities everywhere.

Poster Copyright © 2010 Karl W. Palachuk
Design by Connie Kong

10. Know What You Know

There's a "classic" model for looking at knowledge that's known as the "Conscious Competence" model. It describes the evolution of knowledge about any subject. There are four stages:

1. Unconscious Incompetence. Here, you don't know what you don't know. You might not even know that the subject of knowledge is a "thing" that other people know. You are literally clueless. You don't even know the words to describe what you don't know.

2. Conscious Incompetence. When you begin to learn about something, you realize that there's a lot more to it than you thought. And you can learn more and more, but it all just seems to reinforce the knowledge that there's much more that you don't know.

This stage is essential in your growth and success. It makes you aware of all the things you need to learn. And your conscious awareness of your own ignorance helps you to see the boundaries of your knowledge. You may choose to avoid learning more on a subject, but you are aware that you have made that decision.

3. Conscious Competence. Here, you have learned a certain skill level, and you are aware of where you stand with regard to your knowledge. You know what you know! And, better yet, you know that you have certain knowledge. You can sit down and figure out pretty much everything in your field. If you're not careful, this stage can lead to arrogance.

4. Unconscious Competence. This is (theoretically) the pinnacle: You know so much about a subject that you perform

"automatically" and do not have to think. You have totally internalized the knowledge and become a master in your field.

If you want to learn more, just Google "Conscious Competence." There are plenty of resources out there.

No matter what stage you are at, you can be aware of your own knowledge. Just take a little time to think about it (slow down, get more done) and you'll figure out where you fall. Are you the most skilled person in this field? Top ten percent? In the middle? Beginner?

I encourage you to figure out where you are with regard to the knowledge areas most important to service delivery in your company. Also, encourage your employees to do the same. There are many benefits to this.

When you make knowledge awareness a part of your culture, you also encourage people to be absolutely honest about their self-awareness. This can lead to a culture of constant training, constantly sharing knowledge, and constantly improving the skills of everyone on the team.

In my IT service businesses, I always kept a spreadsheet with the key knowledge areas we valued (e.g., technical skills, troubleshooting skills, customer service skills, etc.). It was actually quite a long list, with a lot of emphasis on the technical knowledge. Then we ranked everyone and listed the top three people in each category. Who has the most knowledge of Internet routing protocols? Firewall configurations? Microsoft Office products? And so forth.

This information allows you to help people set goals. You want to be number one in customer satisfaction? Okay, first get to #3, then #2. We'll make it part of your quarterly goals. We'll get you the time to practice and the training that's needed.

Getting It Wrong

Many companies get knowledge awareness "wrong"— and it hurts them in the long run. How do you get it wrong? There are a few ways.

First, you might have a culture that encourages some people to hoard knowledge in the false belief that it increases their job security. So, one person holds lots of knowledge and many others are hampered in their jobs because they cannot access the knowledge.

Similarly, knowledge hoarding can lead to a lack of training for people who need it. If one person is to be the expert, then others are not trained, even though it would be good for everyone, and the company.

Second, you might find that your company has "silos" of knowledge. That happens when departments feel like they're competing with one another. They don't share knowledge because they want to maintain a certain relationship with the customer, the owner, or even certain vendors. They don't trust other departments, and keeping knowledge to themselves allows them to have more control over the decision-making process.

There are many reasons for knowledge to become siloed. I would like to say that it always happens by accident, but there's too much evidence that that's not the case. Very often, knowledge is siloed for strategic reasons. I do know this: Knowledge silos are always a bad thing and always a sign of a culture that needs to be fixed.

A third way that knowledge awareness can be wrong is called the Dunning-Kruger Effect. Again, Google it. The Dunning-Kruger Effect is a very odd and surprising observation: People who have just a little bit of knowledge actually believe that they have superior knowledge.

In other words, the least knowledgeable people tend to think they are the most knowledgeable!

Think back to the Conscious Competence mode. Some people are in the Unconsciously Incompetent stage (they don't even know what they don't know), but they think they are in the Consciously Competent stage (they think they know it all).

It is surprisingly easy to fight this tendency: Create a culture of knowledge awareness. Make everyone on your team aware of their knowledge level, and the knowledge levels of everyone else on the team. At the same time, encourage people to share knowledge, grow their knowledge, and help each other out.

One of the great truths about life is my personal motto: *Nothing happens by itself.* This is certainly true when it comes to knowledge awareness!

The Benefits of Knowledge Awareness

Aside from all the good things above, knowledge awareness can do a lot to improve your company's successful service delivery. As with everything else, there are several layers to this.

One great benefit is getting improved support when you need it. For example, when your team needs to get support from a manufacturer or service provider, your honest and accurate self-awareness of knowledge helps a lot.

Let's say you call tech support for whatever software you use to run your business. The service provider will try to figure out whether you are a beginner, an average user, or an expert. You need to be honest about this!

When you call tech support, you should always try to evaluate them as well. You should be talking to someone who knows more than you do. That obviously requires that you know where you are. And you can't over-state your knowledge (intentionally or not) because then you slow down your own progress in solving the problem.

If you're talking to someone who knows more than you (very likely), then you need to become the student. Take great notes. Use the call as a learning experience. But if you know more than the person you're talking to, you need to get escalated as soon as possible. Again, you want to be talking to someone who knows more than you.

One way to get escalated is to take extremely good, thorough notes about what you've done and what you have not done. This includes actions you took with the lower level tech support. (As a side note, if you take good notes, you will usually have better notes than the people you're talking to.)

When the support folks realize that you really do know what you're talking about, what you've done, and the order in which you've done it, they will treat you with more respect and together you will solve the problem sooner.

There is tremendous power when you realize that you absolutely master a certain knowledge. This normally comes after many years working with the same information. Don't fool yourself and think you are at a "master" level before you really are!

When you truly master some knowledge, you will be able to assess the situation very quickly. You will be able to make good decisions almost automatically. You may never be perfect, but you will end up being right pretty much all the time.

And before you know it, a dozen years will have passed . . . and you will be Unconsciously Competent.

11. The Competition Is Irrelevant

Let's do an exercise: Bring to mind your largest or most successful competitor. Got it? Make sure you know exactly who you have in mind before you proceed.

Okay, now answer these questions:

- What do they charge per hour?   _____
- How many hours does their average client
  pay them for?   _____
- What is the cost of their core service offering?   _____
- How many clients do they have?   _____
- What's their profit margin?   _____
- What's the average length of their contract?   _____
- How much do they pay their technicians
  (key employees)?   _____

You might know that last one, but the rest of it doesn't matter. I have never paid any attention to my competition for any financial decisions I've ever made in my company.

Here's one reason why.

When I was in junior high, I thought, "You know what I should do? I should go mow lawns on the nice side of town," but I didn't want to drag my lawnmower all the way to the other side of town. So I put an ad in the newspaper that said,

"I will do all your yardwork but you have to supply all the equipment, $5 an hour."

I'm old, so this was 1972. I didn't know that there was such a thing as a minimum wage. I have since looked it up: It was $1.60.

It didn't matter. I wanted to work and $5 would get me off my butt and across town to work on yards. I was paid $5 an hour and I was busy all the time. I always had work because the people who were willing to pay $5 an hour also didn't know what the minimum wage was—and they didn't care.

Here was this kid who was energetic, and he was going to come and mow the lawn, or whatever. Let me tell you: I did some horrible, horrible jobs at $5 an hour. But they paid me in cash and I didn't know about taxes back then either!

You are worth (your products and services are worth) **exactly what someone is willing to pay right now**, today. And there's always someone willing to pay top dollar. You just have to find them!

When I started my first "real" business in 1995, I did basically the same thing. When I first got started as a consultant, I charged $100 an hour. Why? Well, that number sounded big enough to be taken seriously. And I didn't know that in 1995 in Sacramento, California, nobody was charging $100 an hour, except me.

I have always maintained that I want to be more expensive than my competition. Not a lot, but I want to be the most expensive person that you're likely to pick up the phone and call for tech support. This has never affected my ability to get clients.

Important note: It *has* affected who those clients are. I had a lot of attorneys, accountants, and other people who relied on their technology to make good money. For most of the time I did tech support, I had a number of medical-related clients who were very dependent on technology and were willing to pay to keep it going.

When I sold my last IT company, in 2017, we were charging $165 per hour while almost everyone else in town was still around $125.

I'm not saying you need to charge a lot or place yourself at the top of a heap. But *charge what you want to charge* and then find people willing to pay it. But whatever you do, ignore your competition. They don't run their business exactly like you. They don't have the same employees, the same clients, the same business model, etc.

Note: I have definitely not been able to serve clients who fit outside my model. I don't do home networks, for example. So that market never comes to me. And I don't sell used equipment or discounted labor. So those people don't come to me. I don't fix cell phones or deal with high end security systems, drones, audio-video, or "Internet of Things." It's not that I couldn't. I just didn't.

I put together a few simple bundles that made sense to me, that were guaranteed profitable, and I sold them to people who found value in what I offered.

It really is that simple.

Remember the story of two electricians in Chapter 4. One differentiated himself by being cheap. The other by being professional. One was ten times more expensive—and got the job. I wanted peace of mind, and I got that.

Let me tell you one other story about why your competition is irrelevant.

It's about Sally, who managed the business side of a construction contractor. I used to put on educational luncheons, and she attended several. She never asked me about my prices, but she always asked about software and hardware. She made it clear that she had someone taking care of her technology, so she just wanted the education. Cool.

Then one day she asked me to review a proposal and tell her what I thought. I gave her some advice. When she asked what I would charge, she was shocked. It was significantly higher. She asked me how I could get away with that. I just told her that I don't know anything about the details of her business or the skillset of her IT guy. But I know I'm a Microsoft Certified Systems Engineer and we never cut corners.

She didn't hire me that day. But she continued to come to my classes. She actually relied on me for lots of information, which she took back to her IT guy to implement. Then one day, she called me and asked if I provided ongoing services on a contract. I said yes. She asked me to come over and sign one so they could get started.

Here's the funny thing: In that conversation, she didn't ask what my rates were, what the minimums were, or what service we provided every month for our fee. She basically bought the idea of having me take care of her network.

When you make decisions about how you put together your offers, what your bundle looks like, what your core offering looks like, what your pricing looks like, etc.—Please ignore your competition! If they choose to compete with you, the only thing they can really do is charge less. So, your competition will be making less than you while trying to figure out exactly what you do for the money.

Alternatively, they could do lots of research and create a comparison point by point of your businesses. Then they become a copy. But again, without the details, it's not a good copy.

And when you change (add a new product line, incorporate new services, create a new bundle), then you move their target. When you evolve with the times, your so-called competition is now actually in a different business.

As you can see, this whole book is wrapped around an over-arching philosophy:

- Do what you want to do
- Do it the way you want to do it
- Do it with the people you want to work with
- Charge what you want to charge

In other words, do business *your way* and find people who want to do business with you.

12. We Only Work with People We Like

I want to say this is all about work/life balance, but it really isn't. This rule is about productivity, team development, and supreme customer service.

Too many people—maybe even the majority—start out their businesses believing that they have to take every job, take every dollar. In fact, I've read in books the offhand statement that, "when you start out and have to take any job you can . . ." But that's not true!

In the next section, I have chapters explaining why you don't have to take every penny that's offered to you, you don't have to work with jerks, and so forth. Here I want to convince you that you will have a much better, healthier, more profitable business if you choose to work with people you like. And this has the added benefit that you won't get a bleeding ulcer from the stress of a business you created.

Working with people you like will dramatically reduce the stress in your company. You already know that. Think about your favorite client. It makes you happy, right? Now think about your least favorite client. Did your blood pressure just go up? Are you on the verge of telling me what those losers did just last week?

Many, many, many business owners have argued with me about this over the years. They are adamant that they have to work with jerks because they need the money.

Trust me: There are enough nice people in the world that you can base your business on working with nice people! The number of nice people might appear to have gone down recently, but if you get off Facebook and go talk to business owners, it's still a significant chunk of the population.

You really can build a business only dealing with people who are not rude, not arrogant, and not abusive.

The second largest client I ever fired had been with me for about ten years. Our relationship started out super-friendly. They were really great to work with. I remember when my brother Manuel came to work for me and went to this client for the first time. He sent me a text message that said, "Man, these people love you. They will never leave you."

This client was run by a man and wife team. She was always nice to us, but we saw her turn on people and become arrogant and abusive to others. One by one, as they became richer and more successful, she fell out with one vendor (or employee) after another.

Eventually, they became arrogant and abusive of my technicians. I sat them down and I said, "This is a one-strike-and-you're-out kind of thing. You cannot talk to my technicians like that." It did not go over well. They made it clear that they were the boss, they were paying the bills, and they can do whatever they want. I was a contractor and not in charge of this relationship.

So, I wrote them a note and I fired them. That contract was worth about $75,000 per year. It hurt at first. But this move also dramatically reduced the stress inside my business and let my employees know that they are valuable to me.

Several good things came out of this. First, my employees loved it. They clearly know where they stand—and it's above one of our largest clients. For a few years, technicians would tell that story to new employees. So, you see, the culture begins to perpetuate itself.

Second, because that client had gradually become "difficult" through the years, they were less profitable than other clients. So we took that labor capacity and sold it to other companies for more money. And, third, of course, we reduced the stress inside our own company. Part of it was the stress of working with that client, and part was the stress of worrying that we would continue to work with such clients.

This applies to more than clients. We only work with employees we like, suppliers we like, vendors we like.

This rule is difficult to apply when you first choose a company to work with because most companies are very nice and loving before you sign a contract. Every once in a while you'll see a company that just turns you off. If you start to feel uncomfortable and think, "I really don't like how they do business," that's a good sign that you really won't like working with them three years down the road.

When you build a culture where you work with people you like, your employees start projecting that to each other and the world. I remember when my company had about twelve employees, and we were really in a groove with great clients and great employees. One day, someone walked into the office and spontaneously said to everyone, "God, I love working here!"

And then it became a thing. Almost every day, somebody would walk in the office and say, "God, I love working here!" It made me happy that my team honestly and sincerely loved how we operated, and who we worked with.

So, if you want your technicians to love you, and if you want to make everything in your life better, work with people you like.

One final story along these lines.

One time, Microsoft hired our company to go work with a few select clients. They were trying to figure out a problem with the installation of the original SBS Essentials product, which became Windows Essentials. They hired us to try to figure this out, and they sent us three or four clients. We ran through the install again and again and again. We did eventually document both the problem and the solution.

One of the companies that they sent us had an on-site manager who had to get everything approved by the owner. Mike and I showed up for our appointment and this guy brought us into his office. He said, "Let me call the boss. I know that he wants to be here when you guys are here."

So, he calls the owner on a speaker phone and says, "The guys from Microsoft are here." And his boss immediately blurts out a massive blue streak of swearing,

"You stupid son of a blah, blah, blah, blah, blah! You know I wanted to be there. What the hell? What kind of a moron are you?" etc.

He just exploded on this poor manager, who then had to interrupt and tell him he was on speaker phone. Imagine how that went.

Mike and I looked at each other and we knew instantly that this was not going to be our client. No question. We will do this job, but we won't even ask them if they want to sign a contract. They will never be our client.

You really can make this easy. There are enough nice people in the universe. You don't have to build a business working with jerks. In another chapter we'll revisit the false belief that you have to pick up every nickel you find.

Note: As I look back at the last two decades, this truth remains. Even in two nasty economic downturns. You just don't have to work with jerks.

Section IV
Rules for Client Management

13. Define Your Ideal Client—and Go Get Them

14. Don't Have Both Sides of the Conversation

15. You're Not Responsible for Every Lost Dog that Shows Up on Your Doorstep

16. We Cannot Care More about the Client's Network Than They Do

17. Every Client Is on a Service Agreement

18. Evaluate Your Pricing Once a Year

13. Define Your Ideal Client—and Go Get Them

In the last chapter, I talked about working with people you like. In future chapters I'll talk about other aspects of customer management. Here I want you to create a picture of your "perfect" client.

If you haven't done it before, this might sound a bit silly, but you need to create a model client profile. Who is your client? Male or female? Age? Occupation? What is their personality like?

You might create two model clients: One male and one female; or one twenty-something and one forty-something. Define who you will sell to, and define every detail you can think of.

Once you have a very clear focus on your model clients, then you can go and find them. What are their challenges, dreams, and opportunities? And most importantly, why will these clients do business with you? What do you offer that they can't get anywhere else?

Chances are very good that you already have some clients, so let's start there. Make a list of your clients. You might be able to spit this out of QuickBooks or some other program you use. If you are worried about having your client list printed out, assign three- or four-letter codes for each client, so you can identify them.

Now make a list of the things that are important to you. As you know from the last chapter, I only work with people I like. So, one of my criteria is "Good to work with" or even "Nice."

Other criteria might include:

- Profitable
- Interesting projects
- Take our advice
- Right size (measured as money, employees, or something else)
- Pay on time
- Don't ask us to stretch the rules
- They view [the services we provide] as valuable

If you're not sure what to put on this list of criteria, start by bringing to mind your absolutely favorite client. Why are they your favorite? When you find yourself saying "Every client should be like them," that's probably your favorite client. With luck, you have several of them.

Once you've created YOUR criteria (don't just copy mine), you can create columns for these and rate each one of your clients. You might rate them high, medium, or low. Or you might go for a scale of one to five or one to seven. I recommend an odd number so you can copy out and put some people right in the middle.

In the downloads for this book you'll find a "Client Impressions" Word document. It gives an example based on a handful of criteria measured from one (bad) to five (good). You might prefer to put all this in Excel. Use whatever works for you. Finally, there's a total column. This way, you can rank your clients based on the criteria you decided were important.

Any surprises? Is your best client at the top and your worst client at the bottom? They should be.

Why This Is Important

Many people simply won't go through this exercise. They'll take sixty seconds and go through a mental exercise, but they won't really sit down and dig into defining an ideal client. But you should go through this, because it really works.

Once you have a clear picture of your ideal client, you can design products and services perfect for them.

Imagine: What if the next five new clients looked like your best five clients? And what about the next five after that? You can make that happen!

I've done this. In fact, lots of companies have. You can build a business around your absolutely favorite clients. Trust me—it's pretty amazing. But you CAN do it.

Here's where the juicy goodness happens: Imagine what you could do if every single client was like your top five best clients. What would they want? How much would they pay? How can you serve them once you stop worrying about the bad clients at the bottom of the list?

Between the list above and the criteria on my Client Impressions document, you can guess what I was looking for. I went through this exercise every three of four years—for more than two decades. The result was that I got pickier and pickier—and my clients got better and better.

I offered services that appealed to my best clients. As I went out and got more clients, I attracted people who want those kinds of services. So, over time, my clients actually became ideal. The system really does work. Maybe not overnight, but eventually.

I sometimes joke that I started my last IT business by accident. I had sold my business about five years before. And the guy who bought it had sold it again. But the new-new owner just didn't have a good "small business" mentality. He thought he could provide half-baked service and get away with it. But remember who my clients were: They were willing to pay top dollar, but they also expected top-shelf service.

Over time, one client after another came to me and begged me to take them back. Time and time again, I told them I'm not in that business anymore. Then, one day, a former client called me in a panic. The new consultant had done something that broke every single thing in their business.

I thought that was an exaggeration. But she was in a panic, so I went down to her office. The firewall was messed up. The server was messed up. Email wasn't flowing. The web site was down. The backup was broken. Remote access was broken. Finally, I had to admit: He really had broken every single thing.

It's a long story I'll tell you someday when you buy me a beer. But for the technicians in the crowd, here's what happened.

First, he had updated the firewall without backing up the configuration. That seemed to "break" all the other functions. But rather than fix the firewall, he proceeded to assume that something had gone wrong on the server at the same time. So, without fixing the firewall, he started messing with the server. And then the email, the web server, etc. He went and broke each of these one by one because it never occurred to him that his firewall update was the actual culprit.

Remember that chapter on Know What You Know? He did not know that his one action started this snowball rolling downhill. And I *did* know that all these things can't just break at once unless there's a single cause.

Anyway, at that point I was looking at a few hours' labor. I told my former client that she was not alone. There were a handful of former clients who had already fired this guy and had been calling me. I told her, if I can get five perfect clients signed up, I'll go back into the IT business. And so, I did.

Imagine how awesome that business was. I only took ideal clients. Every one of them took my advice, spent money when I told them to, paid their bill on time, paid top dollar, replaced their equipment before the warranty was up, and treated me with respect. And it gets better. Because they all did exactly what I told them to do, their equipment just worked. Things didn't break. They didn't have downtime. They were supremely happy—and so was I.

I promise you: This is not bullshit. Yes, it took a long time. But even before it was perfect, it was well on its way. The business I sold many years before was the root stock that helped me build the perfect business in the end.

To be honest, this rule—Define Your Ideal Client—is a great example of both the puzzle analogy and the Pareto principle from earlier. This rule will work slowly over time. Think "tortoise" and not "hare." As you begin gathering amazing, perfect clients, you will move into offering the things they want and need. Your business will morph away from trying to please everyone to trying to please ideal clients.

In every other client discussion in this book remember the ideal client. All those puzzle pieces fit together.

14. Don't Have Both Sides of the Conversation

I know you're smart. And you probably know you're smart. But you're never so smart that you actually know what other people are thinking, no matter how long you've known them.

Way back when I wanted to start my first business, my wife was a state worker and had the perfect state-worker view of employment. She had a job where she could never be fired. She had guaranteed income for the rest of her life, a retirement plan, and felt comfortable that the bills would be paid every month. She had security in her job.

As a result, I was afraid to have a conversation with her about quitting my really good, well-paying job to start my own business with zero clients and zero dollars coming in. I worried about this conversation for months. Finally, I just had to have the conversation. We sat down and I told her I wanted to quit my job and start a consulting company. I was prepared to answer all her questions about what it would look like, how I would get my first client, and so forth. Her response was, "Okay."

Wait.

What?

I was surprised how easily she went along with the idea. I told her that I know how much she needs security, etc. She said, "I need that for me. You can have whatever level of security that's comfortable for you."

I put off this conversation for months because I had both sides of the conversation in my head.

How many times have we done that? Whether it's a difficult client, a vendor, or our kids. When you have both sides of the conversation, you don't give the other person the opportunity to give you their actual response. You assume you know what they'll say, and you make it more complicated than it needs to be.

How does this natural human tendency (to have both sides of the conversation) show up in your business? I've worked with many business owners and I see it all the time.

One great example with service companies is the belief that "My clients would never sign a contract." Really? They sign contracts with everyone else. You can't get a cell phone or an office lease without a contract. Business owners convince themselves that their clients want to do business a certain way, primarily because it reflects *their* beliefs, not necessarily their clients' beliefs.

Other examples include, "My clients won't pay in advance." Or, "My clients won't pay with a credit card." But you can easily see that they pay in advance for many things, and they certainly pay with credit cards all the time.

Until you ask your clients, you don't know.

With all service delivery (no matter what your company does) I highly encourage people to get paid in advance whenever possible. There's one conference I attended two or three times a year for about five years. Time and time again, I encouraged everyone to get paid in advance for everything. I would say, "You can do this starting right now."

Time and time again, someone would hear that advice and, the next time I was up on stage, they would give testimony to the crowd: "I took your advice. I didn't believe that it would work. But I had zero resistance. Clients just paid up front."

In that testimony, they admitted that they had this conversation inside their heads, but as soon as they included the clients, they discovered there was no resistance.

I encourage you to take inventory. What beliefs do you "know" about your clients that aren't true?

When you have to have a difficult conversation, avoid playing it over and over in your head. Just go have the difficult conversation and you'll probably find that it's not difficult at all.

How to Apply This Advice

Whenever you hear advice and your first reaction is,

- "That doesn't apply to me"
- "My clients wouldn't go for that"
- "I can't get paid in advance for everything"
- "That goal is unrealistic"
- "No one would do that"
- "No one would pay that"
- "If I raise my rates, this client will fire me"
- etc.

All that automatic resistance is you having both sides of the conversation.

Before you accept that first impression, step back a bit and let the other party have their half of the conversation. Your clients are open to all kinds of things you haven't tried. Just ask them! The same is true with your employees, vendors, distributors, manufacturers, families, and clients.

Don't have both sides of the conversation!

15. You're Not Responsible for Every Lost Dog that Shows Up on Your Doorstep

When you're in a service business, you have to make sure there's a good match between the services you offer and the clients you serve.

Way back in Chapter 4, I told the story of the two electricians. One was obsessed with the cost of services. He was willing to do a marginal job and make a very small profit in order to simply have a client. I was not a good fit for him. I'm the kind of person that would rather pay a little more, have the job done right, and eliminate re-work before the work starts. The second technician focused on quality first. I'm a much better fit for that approach.

When you have a good sense of who your clients are, you need to accept that many people do not fit your model. Do not feel bad about that. You should not try to help them unless you have a strong belief that they will become your target client. And do not worry that "someone" has to help them. You might even help them find that someone, but you should not lose sleep over the fact that they are not your ideal client.

Here's a common scenario from my IT consulting business. People will call out of the blue and ask me to fix their computer. But they have never hired me before, and they haven't actually maintained their computers. Everything about the job makes me see big red flags: Avoid at all costs!

My ideal clients see their technology as an investment. They consider it vital to their business, so they hire a person or company to take care of their computers. When they call, I am happy to go talk to them about how we can help.

But when someone calls and they clearly place no value on their technology, I know every discussion will be about money. And they will think I'm over-charging for everything. That will not be a good relationship, so we need to walk away.

No matter what business you're in, there are many people out there who literally cannot afford your services. Don't try to serve people who cannot afford you. And don't feel bad about it. You and your customers will both be happy when you are a good fit for each other. Remember: Even if you gave great service to someone who really didn't want to pay that much, they will repay you by complaining about your company at every opportunity. That's not good for you in the long run.

You should figure out the annual cost of your services and have a very realistic vision of who can and cannot afford you. Don't sell to people who can't afford you. For example, in IT support, a company that brings in $300,000 a year (total revenue) cannot afford to pay for ongoing preventive maintenance of their technology. They don't have enough free cash to pay us enough money to make it worth our while.

What is the minimum size a company has to be to afford your services? Whatever it is, you should make a note and then figure out how to go get clients who are at or above that threshold. Stop trying to sell to people below that. Don't lower your rates to try to get clients who aren't a good fit in the long run.

Here's an exercise to help find (and possibly remove) clients who are too small for your services.

Open up your QuickBooks, or whatever financial software you use, and you run a report of *sales by customer*, summary, for the last twelve months. Next, sort that report from highest to lowest and start drawing some lines.

Look at all the people that gave you $250 or less in the last year, or under $1,000 dollars last year. How big is your average client? What percentage of your revenue comes from the top twenty-five clients vs. the bottom twenty-five clients?

No matter what business you're in, smaller clients take more work per dollar earned than large clients. It's just a fact of life. If you drop the smallest ten clients, would you notice the difference in revenue, or would you just sell those hours to someone else for more money?

As I've mentioned before, you need to start looking at your ideal client. I'll bet that your five favorite clients are at the top of the list, not the bottom. Those really small clients are expensive for you to have on your books. There is a minimum cost to having a client.

I love studying business models and one of my favorite examples is Costco. Costco has a very specific business model. They looked at what grocery stores do and said, "We don't want to do that." When you go to a grocery store, they're happy to have you come in eight times a day, buy a stick of gum, and put it on your credit card.

Costco looked at that model and said, "It costs us money whenever one of our employees interacts with a customer." So, what did they do? For starters, they charge people to get in the door. You have to pay for a membership. They literally have somebody standing at the door who keeps you out unless you are a member of the club.

Next, there's no signage. There is a certain rotation of what they carry on a given day. For you, that means you have to go back and forth, up and down every single aisle. You get the twelve-pack of studded snow tires, you get the ninety-six rolls of toilet paper, and you spend three hundred dollars with every visit.

And you show up once a month.

That's their business model. They do not want you in that store every day. They want you there once a month to spend $300 or $400. As a result, they have far fewer people coming into their store than the grocery store does, but they are far more profitable than the grocery store.

I encourage you to open your mind to new ways of looking at your clients and your business. Create any business model you want and then go find clients who want to do business that way. I've mentioned this before, but it's important: Create *your* business model and then find people who want to do business your way.

You don't have to serve everyone.

This is also true with employees. You're not responsible for every person who shows up looking for a job. Sometimes, the folks who show up really need the work, but they don't have the skills. If you have technicians who are just wasting your time, they're also wasting your money. There is nothing more expensive in your business than labor, so if you have people who are not performing, I'm sorry but—it's really a hard thing to do the first time—you need to weed your employee garden and get rid of those who are not performing.

16. We Cannot Care More about the Client's Network Than They Do

There is sometimes a struggle between what customers want and what they are willing to pay for. I want my yard guy to also trim the back bushes once a year. But that costs extra money. Will he do it for free just because it looks like a disaster area? No. Of course not. He can't care more about my yard than I do.

In the IT business, we always have clients asking to somehow "make" the server live one more year. And then one more. That attitude is fine in the middle of a recession. But you can't escape the trade-off: Old equipment is slow and insecure. Eventually, it just has to be replaced. But that costs money.

I generally sell firewalls that cost in the range of $1,000 to $3,000 for small businesses. But I've had clients who see a so-called firewall at Best Buy and tell me they won't spend more than a hundred dollars. I have to simply tell them that I can't do that. It would not be business class, it would not have the features they need, and it would not be good for their business.

Sometimes we need to walk away from these clients.

There is a point at which we have to draw the line. You cannot lower your prices simply because the client doesn't place value on what you do. In fact, there's irony in the fact that you would consider giving a price break to someone who doesn't care, simply because you insist on helping them to get the right setup. You cannot care more about their stuff than they do.

The biggest example recently has been HIPAA, the Health Insurance Portability and Accountability Act. Doctors who refuse to be HIPAA-compliant are unintentionally making their IT providers liable for hundreds of thousands of dollars in fines. The doctors think no one cares, or that they will never be a target. But the law holds the IT provider responsible even if the doctor doesn't care. You cannot care more about their network than they do.

IT providers need to walk away from those clients simply because the liability is so high. It costs money to be in business, right? And the people who won't spend that money actually cost you a lot more to support because they're the clients having all of these problems.

Maintenance is the same with computers, air conditioners, and cars. You can pay for the maintenance or pay for the fix. But I know this: If I refuse to get the maintenance done on my car, the dealership won't give me a break on the cost of fixing it!

Matching how much the client cares about their business with how much you care is also a good indicator of whether you will consider them a great client. My single favorite client of all time was a woman named Janet. Why? Simple: She always took our advice and followed the "roadmap" process we set up to create a strategic approach to her technology. When we say to replace every machine after three years, she does it. When we say to move to the cloud, she does it. When we say they need a new firewall, she buys one.

Another favorite client is Debbie. Her company does marketing for new home developments. In the big housing recession of 2009-2010, they were hit pretty hard. One day, she called and told my brother (who was president of my company at the time), "You need to help us figure out how to save money."

My brother said, "Well, that's easy. Here's what you're going to do. Give us your server. We're going to stick it in our rack and we're going to have everybody hook up to it remotely. Stop paying your office rent. Send everybody home. You've got all that expensive rent in the Bay Area. It's going to go away. We're going to hook everybody up to work remotely. One day your server will become virtualized. You don't know what it means. It doesn't matter. One day it will disappear altogether. You won't know what that means and it doesn't matter. Everything, we promise you, will work every day as well as it does now or maybe even better."

He literally advised her to shut down her office and let everyone work from home. And she did. Even after selling my business, I still get a check every month because Debbie still pays her phone bill. And those are the kinds of clients you want: They care enough about the services you provide that they will take your advice and commit to paying what it takes to be in business. And sometimes you'll end up saving them a lot of money because you will propose solutions they would never think of.

Here's the ultimate question: Does a client see your service as an **expense** or an **asset** to their business? If a prospect sees your service as an expense, they are not a good fit. Period. You need to walk away.

When a prospect sees your service as a way to contribute to their success, you know they're a good client. When you walk in the door and they say, "This person contributes to my success," then you know you're a part of their team. That's what you're looking for!

17. Every Client Is on a Service Agreement

If your business has clients you serve on a regular basis, this is critically important: All of them should sign an ongoing service agreement (or contract) with you.

What? "My clients would never sign a contract." Please go re-read Chapter 15: Don't have both sides of the conversation!

Here's the deal with service agreements: **Service agreements aren't about service**. Service agreements are about your *relationship with the client* and you and the client's relationship with the government.

It is always the case that, when you're doing business with somebody, your personal stuff and their personal stuff need to be separated. It's also the case that the government has very clear requirements for what constitutes an *employee* versus a *contractor*.

You never want the government to go to one of your clients and say, "You need to start withholding taxes from that account because we deem this person to be an employee and not a contractor." A service agreement separates those things.

The actual services, whether it's a project, an installation, ongoing maintenance, etc., is part of the Statement of Work. It is literally stapled to the end of the Service Agreement. The SOW is not, strictly speaking, the important part of the contract.

The contract/service agreement is about the relationship. It's about how you collect money. It's about what happens when the relationship is over. It's about your legal relationship and your tax relationship. It is not about whether or not you're going to charge $X an hour for work after five p.m.

Contracts help you (and the client) define the relationship. No matter what country you live in, there are lots of laws, and in most Western countries, lots of court cases, that define contract relationships. Lots of these laws, plus all the associated rules and regulations, put limits and requirements on the relationship.

But here's the good news: Many of these laws and regulations specifically state that you can make decisions for yourselves if you sign a contract. For example, a state may limit the amount of interest you can charge on past-due balances—unless the two parties have signed a contract that sets a higher limit.

You need to sign a contract so that you can decide what the relationship looks like, rather than leave it up to the government. So, everybody signs a service agreement.

Red Velvet Rope

The other beautiful thing about a service agreement is that you can use it as a red velvet rope. You know, when you go to the fancy club. The well-dressed dude at the door looks you up and down, and says, "Oh, you want to get in? I'm sorry, you're not beautiful enough." (Okay, maybe that's just me. But that sort of thing really happens.) Here's your red velvet rope: A client who will not sign a service agreement doesn't get in.

There are a *few* people in the world who just are never going to sign a contract. To be honest, I'm suspicious of those people.

You have a contract to park your car. You have a contract when you go into a public swimming pool. Trust me, you sign hundreds of contracts per year, some intentionally and some not. But your life is governed by contracts—just do this.

It's a formality that needs to be taken care of, especially for liability reasons. If one of your technicians drops something on somebody's head, you better have insurance.
And it would be great if you had a contract.

18. Evaluate Your Pricing Once a Year

I used to feel like a lone wolf on this issue. Twenty years ago, when I asked a crowd how many had raised their prices in the last five years, almost no one raised their hand. Today, you hear the advice almost universally that you should raise your rates every year.

I'm going to back down from a blanket recommendation. You don't have to raise your rates every year (but, if you do, I'll support you!). I highly recommend that you evaluate your pricing every year.

In fact, you probably have several prices. There's the price of equipment, the hourly labor rate, and bundled service pricing. You might have five or six different kinds of prices. Personally, I think it's a bit much to raise every price every year (but, if you do, I'll support you!).

In some ways, this conversation leads to a complicated decision tree. Did you raise your hourly labor rate last year? Then perhaps you will raise a bundled service rate this year.

I remember that we raised our hourly labor rate in January of 2008. It was a normal increase and we got no push-back. And, in many ways, we were just lucky. The U.S. economy began to crumble in October of 2008 and the global economy followed suit shortly after. There's no way we were going to raise rates in 2009 or even 2010. But we *did* re-configure our service offerings and raise rates within those offerings.

The interesting bit about that era is that we were mostly selling bundled services. So, while raising the hourly rate might have resulted in significant push-back, the re-bundling of services made the increase a lot less visible—and a lot easier to sell.

Now, I have to admit that I totally love Excel spreadsheets. So, I am happy to spit out reports from QuickBooks, pull them into Excel, and play with the numbers as I speculate about how price changes will affect income. You might not love this as much.

But you should revisit your pricing at least once per year, whether you like it or not!

I find that rotating through my service offering makes this much easier for me. I raise hourly rates one year, then service bundles the next, and project pricing the third year. In this way, no one price goes up every year.

Please: Remember not to have both sides of the conversation!

When I tell people to raise their rates, the almost-universal response is that "My customers wouldn't put up with that." This is not true! Your customers put up with rising costs for rent, labor, parts, shipping, cleaning, and almost everything all the time.

Raising rates really is a normal part of business. Please don't have both sides of this conversation. Doing so will always cost you money. Here are a few things to consider.

First, do you have "automatic" rate increases built into any piece of your business? Generally, such increases are good. But, remember that most will be based on some norm or average from the past— for example, a 3% annual increase.

If current inflation is super low or super high compared to your automatic increase, you might be out of alignment with the rest of the market. If you actually look at the increase each year, you might choose to skip a year, have a smaller increase, or have a larger increase in order to stay in line with your industry.

Second, how is the national or global economy? As a rule, I don't want you to pay *too much* attention to the larger economy, but in this case it can be helpful. If there's a recession, you might need to be more strategic about price increases.

I'm releasing this book in mid-2020. The official recession is just starting and no one knows how long it will last. I've recently talked to two different business owners with opposite approaches.

One is choosing to keep prices stable this year and tentatively raising them next year, if the economy improves. The other assumes that getting new business will be difficult this year, so she's raising rates now so that "rate increase" will be old news when the economy does pick up.

Both of these strategies are good, for one simple reason: The business owners thought about it, looked at their numbers, examined their businesses, and made a decision that feels good for them.

Third, look at what you did last year. If you don't want to raise your hourly rate every year, then you'll need to track increases and space them out. Again, I like the idea of rotating through various elements of the business.

Fourth, what is your vision of where your pricing fits in the overall market? Some people choose to market themselves on price. That rarely means expensive. As a rule, those folks look around at their competition and make sure they are cheaper.

A handful take the "expensive" route. I can't say I want to be the most expensive in my market, but I always want to be at the high end. I want to scare off buyers who are cheap, and I want to project a sense of quality and higher-level service. To the extent that pricing affects these factors, it becomes part of my brand.

Fifth, consider whether you really have a choice. Sometimes, the market goes crazy for certain equipment, certain parts, or even labor. Sometimes you have no choice: You can either lose money or raise your rates.

I am shocked at how many people choose to lose money, fooling themselves that this is a temporary situation. You never know when something will move from temporary to permanent. And you should never knowingly lose money on some piece of your business.

I know that someone wants to jump in with a "loss leader" example. The great, mythical loss leader is an offer that loses money in the hopes of sucking in the customer and making more money in the long run. I call this mythical, because every example I've ever investigated showed a different story.

For example: Car dealerships might offer to "lose" $100 or $200 on a sale. You can do the research, find out their true costs, check out the competition, etc. And, sure enough, it looks like they're losing money.

BUT there's a trick! When you dig a little deeper, you learn that the dealership is on the verge of crossing some major sales threshold. It might be ten million dollars of sales in a certain time period, or number one sales in the country for the quarter. Whatever it is, it comes with a major bonus to the salesman or the dealership that far exceeds the $100 extra in your pocket.

If you buy equipment in large quantities, you may have some similar strategies. Call your sales rep on the last day of the quarter and ask what they need to get to the next bonus level. They will sell their stock at a loss to get their extra, super-duper bonus.

My point here is: Loss leaders are almost never a loss. They just look like it because you don't know the details. And, in almost every "successful" example of a loss leader, the numbers are huge—and unattainable by the average small business.

So please do not get in the habit of losing money and tell yourself that you're playing a game that takes a lot more zeros than your current level of operations.

You've heard the old joke, "We lose money on every sale, but we're going to make up for it in volume." That joke persists because there are lots of people who actually believe it can be true.

Pricing strategy does not have to be complicated or sophisticated. In fact, it should be as straight-forward as possible. But you *should* spend a decent amount of time thinking about your pricing.

Here's a bit of bonus truth for you: **The easiest way to make more money is to raise your rates.**

As simple as that sounds, bring it up at a networking meeting and you'll find yourself in a lengthy, bitter discussion. Pricing goes straight to the heart of profitability, and most people spend too much time taking advice from people who don't know anything about their business.

You know your business, your products and services, and your clients. Make thinking about your pricing a regular part of your annual management strategy.

Pricing is never "set it and forget it."

Section V
Rules for Managing Employees

19. Have an Administrative Assistant

20. Have a Formal, Detailed Hiring Process

21. Hire Slow; Fire Fast

22. Culture Is Built from the Top Down

23. You Can't Control People
(But You Can Control Your Processes)

19. Have an Administrative Assistant

Most businesses make a common miscalculation when it comes to their "first hire." And even after ten or fifteen years, many still continue to make the same miscalculation.

I mentioned Michael Gerber's excellent book *The E-Myth Revisited* earlier. If you haven't read that yet, do yourself a favor and get it. Anyway . . .

Gerber talks about the most common scenario for starting a business: You're good at something (such as baking pies) and you decide to start a business. In his terminology, you have good technical skills and then have an "entrepreneurial seizure."

But, despite your entrepreneurial seizure, you are fundamentally a technician. And that leads you to put technical prowess ahead of everything. That tendency leads you down several bad roads.

One bad consequence of this tendency to focus on technical prowess (in my opinion) is that entrepreneurs tend to get muddled between running the business side of their business and running the technical or service delivery side. Here's how this commonly plays out.

Early on, you have some success. After all, you got into this business because you're awesome and people love what you do, and how you do it. Good job.

Next, the business grows naturally. People love you. They love your work. They send their friends and neighbors. At some point you get more work than you can handle.

Here's where the technical bias comes in.

The most common early mistake of a business is to *hire another technician*. Why? In part it's because that is—by definition—the service delivery that brings in all the money. That's what the business does. So, it makes sense to get someone to help do more of what the business does.

But that decision is almost always a mistake, for several reasons. First, it can be really expensive. If you cannot hire someone part time, or just a few hours at a time, then you have to come up with a regular payroll. You have literally doubled the size of your business in one move.

Payroll is, and always will be, the largest single expense in your company from now on.

Yesterday, you needed to sell enough to pay yourself and make some profit. Now you need to pay someone else, then pay yourself, then make profit. And, trust me, that's the order almost every business owner starts to think in. Profit has somehow moved to third priority. Paying someone else has moved to first priority.

But you don't have twice the business you had yesterday: You have just enough more that you feel you can't do it yourself. You've dramatically increased costs but you haven't doubled demand.

Hire an Admin First

Here's a different strategy to consider: Hire an administrative assistant or a bookkeeper first. This has several advantages, all of which put more money in your pocket.

First, either an administrative assistant or a bookkeeper can be hired for a lot less money. Very commonly, these folks will work one day per week, or ten hours per week, or twenty hours per week. So you don't have to commit to a full-time salary.

Second, it's amazing what a good administrative assistant or a bookkeeper can do for you. Among other things, they can:

- Make sure bills get put into the system. Now, you can open QuickBooks and see what you owe at a glance.
- Work with the accountant to make sure you're using QuickBooks properly
- Balance the checkbook
- Collect the mail from the mailbox store or post office
- Post payments and deposit checks
- Print up all the invoices for review
- Send invoices
- Make collection calls, so you don't have to
- Print newsletters and marketing letters—and send them
- Help organize and execute marketing events or mixers
- Send out packages as needed
- Keep track of all the office supplies. Order supplies as needed.
- Handle new employee paperwork
- Process payroll
- Proofread everything
- Deal with the landlord when something breaks
- Document your processes and procedures
- . . . and so much more!

Now, you might not need all that stuff right away, but you will eventually.

Let's go back to the proper role of technical prowess in your company for a minute. The reason you are tempted to hire a technician is that you really are the single most valuable thing your clients are buying. As a result, every hour of your time that can be freed up will make you more money. You might spend that hour delivering service—at full price. Or you might spend that hour making sales and bringing in more customers.

In either case, an administrative assistant automatically pays for herself (or himself) by *freeing up your time*. At first, it might take two hours of admin time to free up one hour of your time. But it's still a winning calculation.

If you're lucky, you'll find someone who can grow with your company and give you more hours over time. As you make more money and grow the business, there will be a time when you legitimately need to hire another technician.

Again, it would be great if they worked part-time. But in many professions, you just can't find people who are willing to work half-time when there are plenty of full-time jobs.

But now, with a strong admin, you can cut your hours and spend that time doing sales—because you have the capacity to take on more business.

Also, this time, you should have some great processes and procedures documented, so it's much easier for the new technical person to delivery your brand of service by doing things your way.

. . . And if you've been in business a long time?

I still think you need an administrative assistant! Think about all the time you spend balancing checkbooks, running payroll, checking mail, sorting paperwork, filing, talking to clients about money instead of projects, shipping, ordering, and following up on everything.

I know many, many people who have just taken this all on themselves and they will tell you, quite convincingly, that it takes almost no time at all. They are fooling themselves.

And they're losing money.

If you track all of your time in a detailed log—and you're honest with yourself—you will easily find that you are spending five to ten hours a week doing "administrative" tasks that are not high-level, valuable work. The work is necessary. But it's not as high value as sales or developing strategy.

And people without administrative assistants or office managers always make less money because of one key function: Invoicing. Business owners who do their own invoicing always forgive money before anyone asks.

If you turn over invoicing to an admin, it becomes a lot more automated. The admin doesn't know that *this* customer has been with you for twenty years or *that* customer really deserves a break because of something that happened five years ago.

No. The admin follows the process. Time goes into the system Invoices go out. Ninety-nine percent of the time, the bills are simply paid. No one complains. No one questions it.

And if some client really does ask for a discount, you can give it. But you will still have extra money from the ninety-eight percent who just paid their bill.

A Word about Part-Time Workers

Finally, I feel obligated to address a complaint I've seen online (although rarely). It is not evil to hire people part-time, particularly administrative assistants, bookkeepers, and office managers. There is an army of people out there looking for part-time work.

Some are college or high school students. Many are stay-at-home parents who are extremely talented and well-educated. These folks often want to get the kids off to school, work for four or five hours, and then be done in time to pick up the kids from school in the afternoon.

Over the last twenty years, I have hired dozens of interns, college students, and parents who are balancing family and finances. One of my favorite admins of all time was a woman named Lana. She started working for one of my companies ten hours a week. Then she went to work for another company I owned ten hours a week (in the same office).

In all, she worked for us for more than five years. We wrote a letter about her work status so the bank would understand the situation and give her and her husband a home loan. Both of her children were born while she worked for us.

On more than one occasion, we begged Lana to come to work full-time, but she refused. She wanted her nice, manageable twenty-hour job. On rare occasions she worked more for some big project. But she was super happy with the half-time work.

Note, please, that you have to filter job applicants. Don't hire someone part-time who really wants a full-time job. That won't work in the long run.

But absolutely don't feel bad hiring people part-time. There's a lot of people who are looking for exactly that. And many of them are trained, certified, and experienced.

20. Have a Formal, Detailed Hiring Process

One of the oddest things I've ever read online was a comment that small businesses should not have a hiring process. The writer argued that small businesses "just hire"—they don't have a process. Bizarre.

Remember: If you do something, you *have* a process. It might not be consistent, organized, or documented. But you have a process. The benefit of documenting your process is that it can become consistent and organized. And that means it can get better over time.

The next chapter is entitled, "Hire slow, fire fast." That's an old adage that mostly applies to the firing part. This chapter is all about the hiring part.

"Hiring Slow" really means hiring carefully. You need a process for hiring. Hiring the wrong employee can be very costly. You will invest time and money into your employees. You will probably invest in their training. And, in a small business, you will probably invest in their friendship.

All of that makes it very difficult and expensive to make the wrong decision.

Every time we've made a bad hire, it was because I (the boss) went outside the process and just picked somebody. Or I short-circuited the process by taking a personal reference and didn't check out the prospect myself. We have a process that works. When we use it, we get great employees. When we ignore it, we get headaches.

You could hire your friends and cousins. You could just offer a job to someone who meets the basic requirements on a resume and hope you get lucky. But those are not "processes" and don't lead to good decisions.

You have two goals here: 1) Make a good hire, and 2) Avoid a bad hire. Hiring the wrong employee can damage your business. Any process that helps you avoid a bad hire is worth doing.

What goes into the hiring process? I think it's helpful to think of a consistent flow from job description to employee evaluation. The pieces (in order) are:

- Written job description
- Job requirements
- Job advertisement
- Candidate screening criteria
- Candidate evaluations
- Job offer
- Quarterly goals
- Quarterly evaluation

You should have a Word document or Excel spreadsheet for each of these. That's the beginning of documentation—and improvement.

Note also that this is an iterative process. That means you'll go through it again and again. Each time you go through this process, it should get better and better. And you don't have to make improvements in the same order. If you think of something in the evaluation process, that can lead to a fine-tuning of the requirements document.

At first, job descriptions will be fairly vague. You might look at other job descriptions in online job listings. But be sure to customize these for your company and your management style or brand.

Job requirements are next because they grow out of the job description. As the job description evolves and becomes more detailed, so will the job requirements.

From these, you will create your advertisements. I *highly* encourage you to customize job postings so they reflect your culture and style. For example, I embed a note in my ads that says applicants get extra points for using the word "stupendous" in their application.

This might sound silly, but it demonstrates attention to detail—and a willingness to be playful in the workplace. Very few people have included the special word and then turned out to be a bad fit with the culture.

The screening criteria go beyond the strict job requirements. Yes, they include things like experience with the subject matter. But they might also include general experience in a small office versus large cubicle farms. People who excel in an office with a thousand cubicles often do not do well in small business.

Evaluations should be simple. I recommend a few key items measured on a five-point scale. That gives you high, medium, low, and a bit of fudge factor. Have everyone who met the job candidate fill out the evaluation. The items where everyone agrees are less interesting than where they disagree.

The job offer is listed here because you should actually have a written job offer. This does a couple of things. First, job candidates take it seriously. Remember, a job candidate might be in the final stages of being hired by someone else at the same time. You want them to put your company first.

The other benefit of a written job offer is that it makes it very clear exactly what you are offering and what they are accepting. True story: I almost hired an office manager once, but had to shut down the process when I realized that she thought my offer of "forty" was for forty dollars an hour, rather than forty thousand per year.

Finally, the criteria that defined the job, the advertisement, and the evaluations should also flow right into the expectations for job performance. So quarterly goals and evaluations are not a mystery and are once again made plain by writing them down.

Whenever you detect confusion in this process, it's a good sign that you should start at the top of the list and make sure that you have clarified your expectations throughout the process, from job description to quarterly evaluations.

None of these documents need to start out big or verbose. Just start with the basics. You will keep refining for the rest of your business life.

Let Your Ad Do the Work

The reason there are entire companies to help you hire someone is that sorting through resumes can be a huge, overwhelming, and depressing job. We have posted ads that have resulted in almost a thousand resumes.

I don't care what anyone tells you, that's overwhelming, and you eliminate people for stupid, petty reasons just to cull the field.

We have tried to make the job posting work for us. That means that some filtering takes place in the process of responding to the ad. For example, my ads always say, "do not send your resume. If you send a resume, we will delete your email."

Instead, we ask applicants to send a paragraph telling us why we should ask for a resume. No exaggeration here: This eliminates ninety percent of potential applicants! It also helps filter *in* people who are a good fit with our culture.

As we begin to sort, we start by eliminating those who are not qualified. That means they have no relevant experience, or clearly do not meet other requirements. This removes most resumes from consideration.

Next, we eliminate people who are just blatantly stupid or not trying.

If their email address is related to drugs or sex habits at AOL.com, we eliminate them. (If you think I'm kidding, welcome to the world of "Human Resources.")

The remaining resumes are divided into "High" and "Maybe" categories. Basically, the highly qualified group is truly first-tier people. They have lots of experience in the field, they've won an award or two, and they've held related jobs for a long time. The Maybe group is people who are clearly qualified but just don't look like superstars at first glance.

If we can hire from the High group, we will obviously do that. But sometimes this group is very small and we don't make an offer in time. The Maybe group consists of qualified people, and is often filled with technicians who are "diamonds in the rough." We have hired a number of these people through the years and we have been extremely pleased with the results.

I won't go into all the details of our hiring process. The main point is: You need a process. You certainly don't have to do it my way, but you should do it *your way*.

If you want to see a great example of a hiring process designed to filter IN people who fit the culture and filter OUT people who won't be successful, *read Delivering Happiness: A Path to Profits, Passion, and Purpose* by Tony Hsieh, the founder of Zappos. One of their criteria is that candidates "be a little weird."

A Few More Hiring Tips

As your hiring process evolves, you will find tools that work for you to get good candidates. For example, you might hold quick phone calls just to see if people have good manners. You might hold three interviews for each candidate, back to back with different members of your staff. That measures eagerness, and gives the candidate a chance to relax into the process.

Over time, you will find questions you really like to ask. As a rule, you want to ask open-ended questions that allow the candidate to dig into their experiences, like, "Tell me about a time you dealt with an upset client."

That format ("Tell me about a time …") is very powerful. Tell me about a big sale. Tell me about getting along with annoying co-workers. And so forth.

Personally, I enjoy taking prospects out to lunch with my crew after a few interviews. This makes them very relaxed. They open up about their hobbies. My employees can get a sense of whether the candidate is a good fit for the team. Plus, I can see how they treat the wait staff.

I also like to give the candidate a homework assignment. We write up a short assignment that allows them to demonstrate that they have some knowledge of the field. We also get to see how well they communicate.

Believe it or not, even after three interviews and a lunch, about half of the candidates simply disappear once they get a written assignment. I haven't done a lot of research to determine what we're eliminating, but I do know that people willing to write a paragraph have been good employees!

There's also a big question you need to ask a candidate every time you see them. I learned this from my friend and coach Josh Peterson:

"What's changed since I saw you last?"

That is a great question to ask anytime you see someone. But it's particularly powerful in the hiring process. Did the candidate's spouse have an accident? Did they accept another job offer?

Leave this very open-ended. If they got a job offer from another company, this is their opportunity to bring it up. Whatever's going on in their life, this is their chance to spill the beans.

Two other great questions that you should ask every serious candidate:

"Is there any reason you cannot work on this job Monday through Friday 9:00 a.m. to 5:00 p.m.?"

And

"If we made you an offer, would you accept it?"

These questions allow you to avoid asking about religion, personal habits, and overly-personal information. But they also allow the candidate to be perfectly honest about what's going on in their life.

Having the wrong employees can be devastating to a business. Having the right employees is like a super power that lets you do amazing things that you never imagined. Whatever your style, create a system for finding employees that maximize your success.

21. Hire Slow; Fire Fast

One of my favorite business authors is Brian Tracy. And my favorite advice from him is: Hire slow; fire fast.

(See, among other sources, *How the Best Leaders Lead* by Brian Tracy.)

The slowest hiring process I've ever been through was with HP in the mid-1990s. I was to be a contract employee (not an HP employee), but I was to manage a team of twenty-five software technicians, plus manage the sitewide backup systems, and the Unix help desk.

I had a couple of initial interviews. Then, some folks flew into town to interview me some more. Then I took some tests and had an interview with my future bosses—from both HP and the outsourced staffing agency.

In all, the process took more than a month. That might be a bit much for many small businesses, but the results were amazing.

I can honestly say that one of my strongest long-term impressions of my time with HP is that they had great people. With one notable exception (on my team), every single person I dealt with there was top-notch.

At one point there was a facility-wide issue (that's about 5,000 employees) with the servers. So a group of managers from various departments was formed to address the issue.

Overwhelmingly, there was an understanding that every single person in that room was qualified, was honest, and was dedicated to the larger goals of the organization.

Your mileage may vary, of course, but my experience was that a high quality, well-executed hiring process resulted in an extremely high-quality workforce.

For my thoughts on hiring slow in a small business, see the previous chapter.

Now let's talk about firing fast.

Remember I said that there was one exception at HP? Well, I was not involved in the hiring of contract workers for the Unix help desk, even though I managed that team.

One day, we got a new Unix programmer. I met him at the front door, got him through security, and got him all "badged up" to work at HP. Then I delivered him to his desk and introduced him around. About an hour later (no exaggeration), I got a call saying that I had to get him out of the building and make sure he never came back. What happened?

At this facility, at that time, there were food carts that would wander up and down the aisles. They would stop from time to time so people could get donuts, bagels, fruit, etc.

Apparently, a food cart came by and this guy went crazy. He pushed through the crowd, threw down some money, and stuffed his face with donuts. He scared people.

Clearly, he was not a good fit for the culture.

Over the years, I have had to fire very few people. This is the only instance that was not related to job performance.

I'm a big fan of giving people a second chance and trying to make the situation better for everyone so that the "troublesome" employee can continue. But sometimes, you just don't have a choice.

But I have to admit: By the time a personnel situation has deteriorated to the point where someone might get fired, the situation is probably unsalvageable.

I have fired or laid off people under two different circumstances. First, as a manager in a company I did not own. Second, within a company I owned.

In the company I did not own, I also did not hire the troublesome employee. But I knew from the first day I started that she was a bad fit, a bad employee, and needed to leave. I tried various things for almost six months before I let her go.

Almost immediately, everything in the office got better. People were happier and more relaxed. The entire team was more cooperative and efficient.

Another quote from Brian Tracy rang through my ears: "The best time to fire someone is the first time the thought crosses your mind." I have read criticism of this approach from a few so-called business gurus. They say this approach is lazy and that managers have an obligation to work hard to accommodate everyone, even to the point of losing money for the sake of one employee.

I have also spent a lot of time with employees from state agencies and large, global companies. They tell stories you can't believe about employees who simply abuse one system after another, as if the world owed them a paycheck in exchange for zero work.

Note: I understand that these stories represent a microscopic percentage of workers for state agencies and large corporations. But that's part of the point, for small businesses.

A corporation with fifty thousand employees can have a few losers that poison the culture and cost the company money. A small business cannot afford even one of these.

When you have only one hundred apples, one bad apple really *can* spoil the lot.

One of the best managers I ever worked with was my brother Manuel. He was the president of one of my companies for several years. He was kind and patient with employees. He was like a father figure, at times teaching, and at other times correcting.

On the rare occasions when we had trouble with employees, he worked with them to deal with the issues. He was a great manager because he worked with them before things got bad for everyone else.

As a manager, you do have certain obligations to your employees. You need to give them training and guidance. You need to correct them when work is bad. But you also have a right to expect dedicated, focused attention to detail.

Managing is hard. And it's always cheaper to "fix" a current employee than to get a new one. So, I absolutely do not recommend that you fire people every time the thought crosses your mind. But I do recommend that you correct quickly.

I have also laid off employees because I had to. I almost wanted to put "had to" in quotation marks. But the truth is that I had to. Every time I have laid off someone, it was because we could not afford them.

In one case, an employee literally lost us one of our best clients. They quit—and named him as the cause. We lost almost exactly his salary in one day. I kept him on for a little while, but we did not replace that income in short order.

This was a case where I should have gotten rid of him sooner, but he had become a good friend and a key part of our organization. Still, it's the only time I've lost a client due to their evaluation of one of my employees.

I probably should have laid him off the first time the thought crossed my mind.

Size Matters

The larger your company gets, the less direct control you have over culture (we'll talk about culture next). And, the larger it gets, the more likely you are to hire someone who isn't a great fit.

There simply are "bad employees" wandering the earth. They take advantage of any employer that hires them. They work less, try less, and complain more. They gossip and bring unnecessary drama into the workplace. Those people really are out there.

Luckily, they are few and far between. And here's the good news: They love large companies. It's easier for them to hide in the middle of a thousand cubicles than in a 250 square foot office.

When your company is small, you have to be extremely careful about hiring. You have to hire very, very slowly. You have to focus a lot on the team and on culture.

That also means you have to correct very quickly. And if you can't correct, you really do need to let them go as soon as possible.

The bottom line is that you have to work really hard to find someone who fits your style, your brand, your humor, your level of professionalism, your customer service model, and everything else. They don't need to be *you*—they can't be. But they need to work well with you and your brand.

Remember, from Part II, that *your brand is everything you do.* That includes your hiring, your training, and your managing of employees. As a result, you need to work hard to hire the right people, and keep them.

But you also need to get rid of the wrong people as soon as you realize that you can't turn them around.

No one likes to fire people, especially your friends. But sometimes, it's the best thing you can do for your business.

22. Culture Is Built from the Top Down

Every company has a culture, whether they "created" it or not. The truth is, you can either let culture grow on its own or you can create it with intention. Another way to say this is that culture either grows from the top down or grows from the bottom up.

If you ignore culture, it will naturally grow from the bottom up. That means a culture of snide comments, greediness, bad service, unhappy employees, and un-loyal customers. The hardest culture to turn around is one you've accidentally created by not paying attention as it evolved.

Before I started my own business, I had to turn around the culture in a few companies as a manager. I know from experience that this can be a challenge. In one case, it required firing someone who was truly committed to the old (bad) culture I inherited. That was actually the first person I ever fired.

She knew that she was a key team member and probably the most knowledgeable person on the team, so she was also defiant and refused to change. I went to the general manager of the company when I decided that this person needed to go. The GM asked me if I understood the impact on the team. I said yes, but assured her that the impact would be temporary and everything would get better fast without this poisonous attitude on the team.

I don't recommend firing someone as a sacrificial lamb just to start turning your culture around. It could certainly backfire if you do it wrong. But in this case, we had a team of about twenty-five people and we'd had many meetings about changes that needed to be made. When I fired the trouble-maker, everyone knew that we were serious, that we'd do what it took, and there was no turning back.

If you have a newer company, or are just starting to hire people, there's an important lesson here. You create culture from the top down by doing what you say and being what you want others to be. You literally lead by example. If you are calm, rational, and respectful, your employees will be as well. If you yell and scream and drive fear into others, your employees will as well.

The other big example of turning around a culture was less dramatic but also more difficult. I inherited a culture of laziness. People on the team would not take on difficult jobs. They ignored the parts of a job that they didn't like. They did lots of things just a little below their skill level. They did not stretch and did not attempt to excel.

In this case, I simply announced that we were putting a premium on fixing everything with the first touch. In other words, people were applauded for closing a service ticket with one visit and zero re-work. The initial response was a lot of "what if" questions about exceptions to the rule and how to move forward when you don't know what to do.

That was actually a lucky reaction for me. It allowed me to start putting in place a series of procedures in response to the various objections. You need to escalate to someone with specific skills? Here's how to engage them. You hit a problem you don't understand? Here's how to get assistance. And so forth.

My response to all objections was to create processes and procedures that showed everyone how to push through and complete the task under any circumstances. The result was that their attitude shifted from seeing only obstacles to seeing fixes.

In the end, that attitude shift raised the technical ability of everyone on the team. They learned better troubleshooting skills, better documentation skills, and better skills for working with others who had specialized knowledge. And as they learned to call on each other for various challenges, they grew together as a team.

Before the shift, people tended to think of themselves in terms of "Me against the system." After the shift, it became "Us against the problem."

The Elements of Culture

Let's back up a minute and define what we mean by culture. I define culture as *the values and habits of a group*. Company culture is, therefore, the values and habits of a company's employees. This sounds very simple, but there are many pieces to an intentional culture (as opposed to one that grows from the bottom up).

Values. The most important element is a set of agreed-upon values. In many ways, you see the values of my company culture reflected throughout this book. Chapter 12 is a great example: We only work with people we like. Employees know what that means. They understand the implications it has on how we conduct business.

Your values could be written out. That's never a bad idea. But don't just jot down something that sounds good. If you're going to write down your values, you need to spend time considering all the possible values you *could* have and narrowing down the list to the handful that are most important to you in your business.

Here's the secret to understanding values: You can never hide your values because they show up in your behavior. For example, you can say you value open communication. But if everyone is afraid to disagree with the boss for fear they'll be yelled at, that's the actual value that's being lived inside the company.

When I was the Site Manager for PC Software Support at HP's Roseville, California plant, our section had a clear statement on the bottom of every form, every PowerPoint slide, and every memo: We place a high value on work-life balance. That is pretty unambiguous.

So, when someone proposed bringing in a team on Sunday to tackle a job, every person in the section had the right to raise their hand

and ask how that proposal was consistent with our stated focus on work-life balance. Note: That doesn't mean we never worked on Sunday. But we *did* have the discussion in the context of the larger commitment.

Processes. Those who've read any of my books are now saying, "I was wondering how he was going to bring processes into this discussion." The very simple truth is that you can never control people, but you can control your process. See the next chapter.

If you respect people, what is the process for them to have a public, open, safe disagreement about something? If you have a culture of friendliness, how do you work that into a tough schedule on tight deadlines?

We've all seen companies that do amazing work under difficult conditions. Understanding the culture that makes that possible always boils down to *how* they do it. How you do things is the definition of processes.

Processes allow you to standardize how people work together. They also bring consistency to all parts of your business. Whenever you answer a question that begins with "How do we," you should write down the answer. That's the beginning of your process.

Communications are also very important. To me, that is part of the process of culture building. You need to write down, agree on, and communicate these processes. And you should have a process for allowing feedback and discussions.

Team or Community. Your company can only start building an intentional culture once the members see themselves as part of the same team, community, or family. When people feel isolated, they cannot feel like part of the team.

Goals must include team goals. In my consulting companies, every single person had the following goal as the first goal on their quarterly goals and evaluation form:

Provide excellent technical support to our clients while contributing to good relationships within [our company] and between us and our clients.

You can see the emphasis is on building relationships. Lots of stuff falls into the broad category of building relationships. It reflects our values and puts the relationship building at the top of what we expect from people.

You build your team in dozens—or hundreds—of ways. You need to keep culture in mind when hiring. You need to have meetings and get-togethers so the team members can get to know each other (individually and as a team).

In our hiring process, candidates are interviewed by the company president, their potential manager, and a few people they are working with. Everyone fills out the same evaluation form. One of the elements of that evaluation is "Good fit with our culture." Whatever that means to the individual interviewers, it's important that we all agree that someone will be a good fit. That's part of maintaining and perpetuating our culture.

Once you begin to build the culture you want, you need to feed it and nurture it. You need to talk about it and everyone needs to hold everyone accountable for it.

Once you figure out exactly what you want your culture to look like (and this can take a long time), an interesting thing happens: You just do it. You execute your values and your culture follows. Remember, you can't hide your real values. So, once you've decided on a set of values and you begin living them, all the employees will see that.

If you value honesty, you'll get honesty. If you value initiative, your employees will demonstrate initiative. If you value humor, you'll find humor among your team members.

Whatever you decide to do with culture, you should talk openly about it. Eventually, you'll see that your clients also see your culture. It will be reflected in how they are treated. They will see your honesty, integrity, and other values. Or whatever behavior reflects your real values.

Personally, I believe culture is the core of making a company truly reflect who you are and how you choose to show up in the world. See, also, Chapter 37.

23. You Can't Control People (But You Can Control Your Processes)

My first book was on processes and procedures. And most of my other books as well!

As I mentioned earlier, the best thing I read when I first started my business was *The E-Myth Revisited* by Michael Gerber. Processes are absolutely central to growing your business, providing consistent high quality, delivering good service, and building your culture.

The very definition of your business is found in your processes.

Now let's take that to the next level. When I say you can't control people, I mean your employees, your clients, your suppliers, or even the people you hire to do specific jobs. People basically do whatever they want.

Let me give three examples: Time cards, the sales process, and hiring.

Time Cards

I can't tell you how many times I've heard people say, "I can't get my technicians to fill out their time card." What? You only have to do one thing to get paid: Do it.

The answer is to create a process where they have no choice. In the IT consulting business, I based pay on the time card in the ticketing system. Techs had to keep track of eight hours per day. It was either time on a service ticket, personal time (e.g., lunch), or internal time (training, meetings, etc.). All time cards had to be correct when you left for the day.

In fact, I had an administrative assistant start her day by examining the time cards for the day before. If there were gaps or overlaps, she rejected the time card and sent a note to the tech to make corrections. The tech was not allowed to do any other work until the corrections were complete.

Once you create the process, you only really have to focus on one thing: Execution! Think about your success in terms of the area of a triangle. The area is determined by the length of the three sides. See the graphic above. The base is your process. It is known and stable.

One side of the triangle is ability or "can do." You will (well, you should) always hire people who can do the work you have hired them to do. So now you have two known sides to your triangle. You have a solid base and you know your people can do the work.

The volume of the triangle—the volume of your success—is determined by employees' willingness to do the work. As strange as it sounds, some employees just don't want to do certain pieces of their job. It might be the paper work, the boring bits, or the tough jobs. Whatever it is, you can still control your processes, even if you can't control your people.

As a side note, you need to get rid of employees who don't come around to doing things your way. Your processes are your brand. They are your business. Your processes separate you from your competition. They reflect your personality and the way you want to do business. When employees do whatever they want, they are not building your brand!

The Sales Process

Another great example of controlling your process is the sales process. Whether you admit it or not, you have a sales process. For many businesses, the sales process consists of:

- Here's who we are.
- Here's what we do.
- Do you want to buy some?

This puts the buyer 100% in charge of the process. All they have to do is say no and it's over.

I'm a big believer in a slow sales process. That means multiple visits, and avoiding the topic of price for as long as possible. In the slow sales process, the first meeting is all about the client. Let them tell you about their business, how they were founded, how they make money, and so forth. Listen intently, especially to their challenges and problems. Take lots of notes.

The second visit is where you discuss what you do, your special training, your team, and the kinds of projects you excel at. Again, avoid talking about money if at all possible. You can even tell the prospect that you needed to learn about them and they needed to learn about you. You end this visit by asking if they would like you to put together a proposal. You might talk about some of the specific details of the proposal—just not money.

On the third visit, you make a presentation that lays out what you heard. These are the problems you need to tackle. Here are the services we offer that can fix your problems. It's also important to point out to them that whatever they've been doing doesn't work. That might be handling things in-house or a previous service provider whom you intend to replace.

You conclude by asking for feedback. Have we defined your needs? Does this solution make sense? Be prepared to make lots of changes to your proposal. After all, you're just learning their business and you want the proposal to be as effective and enticing as possible. Get into the details. But not the price. You end this visit by asking if you can fine-tune the proposal based on this conversation and give them a quote.

Note that you have avoided talking about price until the fourth meeting. This is hard to do. It takes a lot of practice. But it's a great strategy for several reasons. First, you and the prospect actually understand what the other does at a meaningful level. Second, the prospect has invested some serious time here. Third (ideally), the prospect has gotten to know you. They trust you. They believe you can fix their stuff. And they want to do business with you.

If you go outside your process and discuss money early on, you give the prospect information out of context. $100 or $1,000 or $10,000. Whatever it is, the client thinks they understand money, even if they don't understand what you do. So they will try to speed up the process by making a decision based entirely on money.

When you stick with your process, you will have a much higher success rate. You will understand the prospect and they will understand you. And, best of all, your solution will be a very good fit to solve their problem!

If you break this process, the client will often say no for the wrong reasons, primarily because they don't understand what you will do, or they don't trust you yet.

You can't control people, but you can control your process.

Hiring

This is one area where I have gone outside my process several times over the last twenty-five years. And every single time I do that, I get bit in the butt!

We have a very well-defined process for hiring people (see Chapter 21). We have standard job descriptions, standard ads, a set of pre-defined interview questions, and a set of three different interviews (plus a lunch with a prospective employee). We give prospects a personality profile, we make an offer, and we choose a start date.

I will never forget the worst case of breaking my own process. I had started the advertising process when a friend who had been an excellent employee in the past called me. He gave me the name of someone he had worked with in the past and he recommended that person very highly. So I quickly interviewed the dude and hired him.

He turned out to be the single worst employee I've ever had. Normally, when we let someone go, we lay them off. He is the only person I have actually fired, ever. He was caught stealing company data and passing it to our competition, in direct violation of the non-disclosure agreement he signed.

Whatever your process is, please have a good process. Improve it each time you use it.

You can't control people, but you can control your process.

But you have to *follow your process!*

Section VI
Rules for Billing and Finance

24. Control Billing and Cash Flow

25. Get Prepaid for Everything

26. All After-Hours Work Is Billable

27. It's Not Our Responsibility to Save the Client's Money

28. You Don't Have to Pick up Every Nickel You Find

29. If A Client Has A Past-Due Balance, Their Service Is Cut Off

24. Control Billing and Cash Flow

Have you ever had a year where you barely got by, but then found out you needed to pay more in taxes than you expected? That "crunch" is what bad cash flow feels like.

Cash flow is literally all about how cash flows into and out of your business. When it's good (lots of cash is flowing), cash flow can hide a lot of mistakes. It's a bit like having your own private pyramid scheme: New money coming in pays for old decisions that keep money flowing out.

At certain times, like a financial recession, cash can suddenly stop flowing. That can hurt a lot if you're living too much on cash flow. Here are three examples of cash flow: Neutral, good, and bad.

Neutral cash flow looks something like this:

Income—Expenses = $00.00

When income and expenses are about even, you are covering the monthly costs, you are not "losing" money, and you are not saving money. Unfortunately, too many people think that this kind of *living on the edge* is good. It's not.

Even though we call it neutral, this is actually bad. The reason it's bad is that we all have sudden unexpected expenses. And now, suddenly, you have negative cash flow.

Good cash flow looks something like this:

Income—Expenses > $00.00

In other words, once you pay the expenses, there's money left over to go into your savings, retirement, etc. Ideally, that extra bit will be larger than any unexpected expenses that pop up.

Finally, you guessed it, bad cash flow is negative:

Income—Expenses < $00.00

This means that it costs you money to stay in business. It seems hard to believe, but a lot of business owners operate this way. **And the worst part is: They don't even know it!**

You may be wondering; how can anyone be losing money and not know it? The easiest answer is: They're fooling themselves. I bet you're skeptical about that. But remember, human beings are amazingly optimistic.

Before we get into examples, let me add one more note about the "neutral" cash flow above. Neutral almost never is. Unless you are passing through the neutral zone on the way to positive cash flow, neutral is just negative cash flow waiting to happen.

According to the U.S. Federal Reserve, forty percent (40%) of Americans would not be able to pay a sudden $400 expense with cash on hand. That means they would have to borrow the money. Most commonly, that means putting the money on a credit card or line of credit. It may also mean borrowing money from friends or relatives.

(See Federal Reserve's 2018 Survey of Household Economics and Decision Making - https://www.federalreserve.gov/publications/files/2017-report-economic-well-being-us-households-201805.pdf.)

So, one way we fool ourselves is because we think of "borrowed" money separate from the business. The business grows over *here* while credit card debt grows over *there*.

Another common way we fool ourselves is by confusing profit with cash flow. Your business can be profitable and still have negative cash flow.

Profit is not cash flow.

Cash is not profit.

The banks don't help. I'm sorry. That sounds stupid. Of course the banks don't help. Banks exist to take your money and charge you to access it. Most are fundamentally evil and therefore you can never expect them to "help" in any meaningful way.

Banks—and professionally trained accountants—want you to believe that money owed to you is an asset. That means it's good for you and you can count it as part of your company's value. As we'll see in the next chapter, that idea is absurd.

Money owed to you might have value, and might technically be an asset, but it *never* has a value equivalent to its face value. In other words, the money owed to you has a value equal to some number less than 100% of the total money owed to you.

When times are good and everyone has lots of cash flow, that money might be worth 99%. But as soon as cash disappears (think March, 2020), some people will start paying slow—or not at all. Now, suddenly, money is worth 80%, or 60%, or less.

The next chapter is all about why you should get paid in advance for everything, so I'll save the details for now.

But the point is: Banks and accountants want you to have a profit-focused and balance-sheet focused view of your finances. This is really, really dangerous. As Mike Michalowicz points out in Chapter One of *Profit First*, generally acceptable accounting practices are designed to serve the accountant, not the business owner!

Real World Examples

Okay, here at last are two real world examples. The first is regular, monthly cash flow under normal circumstances. Let's say your company brings in about $250,000 per month (add a zero or take one off if it helps you relate better).

With a neutral cash flow, let's say the cash flows like this:

Day 1   Invoices go out for $250,000

                                      Balance: $00.00

Day 10 25% of invoices paid (+ $62,500)

                                        Balance: $62,500

Day 10 Payroll 1 of 2 (- $93,750)

                                        Balance: $-31,250

Note: $31,250 is borrowed from Line of Credit.

                                        Balance: $00.00

Day 20 50% of invoices paid (+ $125,000)

                                        Balance: $125,000

Day 25 Payroll 2 of 2 (- $93,750)

                                        Balance: $ 31,250

Day 30 25% of invoices paid (+ $62,500)

                                        Balance: $93,750

Day 31 All bills paid for month (- $62,450)

                                        Balance: $31,300

Day 31 Interest on line of credit (- $50)

Day 31 Paid line of credit (- $31,250)

                                        Balance: $00.00

Playing this game—borrowing money to run your business—has a real cost. And the reality of these numbers is worse than this example for two reasons. First, most people use credit cards with interest rates much higher than a bank line of credit. Second, a much higher percentage of the borrowed money does not get paid off every month.

People who run their businesses like this end up borrowing $1,000 a month. Or $2,000. Or $10,000.

And the sad truth is, it is very easy to *not* pay back the loan every month. You can easily add interest payments to your monthly expense and ignore the principle.

This is why, fundamentally, neutral cash flow is ultimately negative cash flow. One little thing goes wrong and you are over the line.

I hope you can see that you have to be *markedly cash flow positive* in order to call yourself cash flow positive. That means you sock away enough cash for a failed air conditioner, losing your largest client, or a sudden recession in the economy.

Here's another real-world example: Taxes. I know. Ugh. If you are not good at setting aside the money you need for various tax payments, you still need to come up with it somehow. This includes state, federal, provincial, payroll, and everything else.

If you suddenly have a big tax payment to make, you may write yourself a check from the line of credit for $25,000. The hard truth is, that money should have been set aside in the past after all other expenses. The other hard truth is even worse: Now you have to pay that off in regular installments *and* make the installment set-asides for the next tax payment.

Cash flow can kill your business.

On the next page is a simple weekly report that can keep you in touch with your cash flow. (This is also available as an Excel worksheet in the downloads for this book. See www.absolutelyunbreakablerules.com.)

The process here is very simple. It is 100% focused on actual cash that you actually have in your actual bank. I don't care what's owed to you or what someone might pay you.

Your bank will not accept good intentions when it's time to pay payroll. You'll need cash in the bank.

Cash Flow - ABC Company, Inc.

Cash Flow Report		Updated: August 31, 2021	
		Amount	Cash on Hand
Cash On Hand - Bank Checking		$25,700	$25,700
A / R Hourly Labor	9/10/2021 +	$50,000	$75,700
A/R from Service Contracts	1/0/1900	$200,000	$275,700
A/R from Equipment		$40,000	$315,700
A/P by	9/10/2021	$92,000	$223,700
Payroll due	9/10/2021 -	**$115,000**	$108,700
A / R Hourly Labor by	9/25/2021 +	$35,000	$143,700
A/R from Managed Svc		$25,000	$168,700
A/R from HW / SW		$40,000	$208,700
A/P by	9/25/2021	$85,000	$123,700
Payroll due	9/25/2021 -	$115,000	$8,700

Here's all you need to do:

1) Enter your actual cash on hand right now. Log into your bank and write down this number.

PLEASE do not go down the road of saying, "But I know someone's going to pay me, or I know a check won't clear right away." This is a zero-bullshit activity.

How much actual cash do you have in the actual bank?

2) Which payments do you realistically expect to receive in the next few days before payroll has to be paid? Again, work from hard, cold reality here. The bank also doesn't accept wishes when it comes to payroll.

3) Which bills will you pay between now and payroll?

There's a learning moment here! Just as you have clients who don't pay on time, you might have to delay paying some bills in extreme circumstances. Don't make a habit of it, because that's just another bad road you can go down.

But be aware that you have some flexibility here, when cash is tight. If you really, really, really think you'll get in a check right after payroll, you might choose to delay paying a bill.

I hope this conversation makes you feel uncomfortable. It should.

Here's one of the rules you can never violate in business: Don't run payroll if you don't have the money. Here's a correlate: Don't pay payroll if you can't pay the taxes. That's a road that can land you in jail while someone from the government is living in your house.

Cash flow is one of the single most important things you need to track in your business. Notice that the cash flow worksheet looks at the next TWO payrolls. On the Excel spreadsheet you'll see that the second worksheet looks at the next two payrolls. And on it goes forever.

In my opinion, you should run this cash flow report at least once per week. It should always look at the next two payrolls.

This process will become less important once you have serious positive cash flow. When you get to where your business should be, you'll have lots of extra cash every month. That will go into your retirement account. When that happens, you can slack off a little. But someone needs to look at your cash flow every week.

Remember:

- Cash is not profit
- Profit is not cash
- You need both

In my book *Relax Focus Succeed*, I stress that you get better at whatever you put your attention on. Cash flow is a perfect example. People who ignore it tend to struggle pay period to pay period. They borrow money and can never figure out how to pay it back.

Those who pay attention to payroll tend to *have* money, and stick it in the bank for when they retire.

25. Get Prepaid for Everything

Believe me: I know that about 60% of the people reading this need to go back and re-read the chapter about not having both sides of the conversation!

But here's the very strange other truth: About forty percent of the readers are nodding their heads and saying, "Yes. Obviously. How else would you do in business?"

There are three major categories of sales that you will make, no matter what service business you're in:

1) Parts, hardware, equipment
2) Ongoing services (normally monthly)
3) One-time labor sales

Now, think about how you *buy* stuff. Your hot tub needs a motor. Your sewing machine needs a tune-up. Your car needs tires.

How do you pay? Basically, there are three options: You pay before you get it, you pay "at time of service," or you put it on a credit card and pay whenever you get around to it. Note: To the service provider, that third option is experienced as option one or option two.

The point is: We are used to paying for things in advance, or when we pick them up. So, whether it's parts or service, we pay for stuff when we get it.

Your clients should be the same. Let's break it down.

#1: Hardware and equipment. There is absolutely no reason that you should extend credit here. Yes, most people pay without any problem. But you are still extending credit. And you might be floating a loan in order to deliver equipment before the client gets around to paying for it.

I feel like an old man when I say this, but I have learned this lesson a hundred times over the years. The first time was in high school when I worked at a hardware store.

If you came in and ordered a bunch of pipes or glass cut to specific measurements, we made you pay in advance. If you wanted common measurements (e.g., a half-inch iron pipe one foot long), we knew we would sell it eventually, so we didn't make you pre-pay.

But if you wanted odd, custom sizes, then we made you pre-pay because we might not be able to sell it to someone else. Or we would have to add additional labor to cut it down more, and not be able to sell some at all.

Whatever you sell, I promise you that you won't sell less if you make people pay at the time they order. And the big bugaboo of the twenty-first century—the Internet—makes this even easier. How many things do you order on the Internet that you don't have to pay for in advance?

(Answer: Less than one percent. Maybe zero.)

Every single dollar owed to me by a client who did not pay is because I extended terms instead of making them pay in advance.

The longer you're in business, the easier it is to adopt this rule: All hardware, equipment, software, and special orders must be paid in advance.

If you need a written policy, just copy the previous paragraph. You're welcome.

Next up: Ongoing services. Many, many businesses have started selling "subscription" services. I have subscriptions for my Microsoft Office software, monthly massages, car washes, lawn service, and more. Almost anything you sell can be sold as a subscription service.

When we sell subscription services, we take a credit card and charge that card on the first day of the month. If people cannot pay with a credit card—some businesses insist on check—then they pay three months in advance. So, for example, by the first of January they will have paid for January, February, March with a check.

This process has several advantages, not the least of which is that it's really great for your cash flow. One of the things that happens too much in small business is that we automatically assume that we're going to give people terms. I did when I started my first business, for no reason. Nobody ever asked me. I just sent somebody a bill and I put, "Net 30." I didn't even know why I did it.

Eventually I figured out, "Well, wait a minute, they pay in advance when they go to Dell or IBM or Lenovo or CDW or anybody except me, so we're not doing that anymore," and I had no pushback from clients. Not one client said, "What? Why do you want to do that?"

There was a transition period. The beautiful thing is, during the transition period, you're getting paid for last month and you're getting paid for next month, so you get this influx of cash.

One common thing that happens when you get paid in arrears is that you end up loaning money to your business for the "float" before clients pay. Let's say you give somebody thirty days. Well, after two weeks you have to pay your employees. After two more weeks you have to pay your employees again. And then you get the check from your client.

This assumes they pay on time. Some clients like to pay on the fifty-ninth day because it's not late until it's thirty days late. So, in that case, you paid your employees four or five times.

When that happens, you may be a little bit short and you put something on your credit card or your business line of credit. Eventually, you get paid by the client. But in the meantime, life has happened. As a result, you pay back most of what you borrowed from yourself but not quite all of it. Now you have a little extra debt that gets carried over. And then it happens again and again and again.

And I have known business owners who were owed $30,000 or more from their clients. One guy I talked to had a client that owed him $70,000. That's one client. I said, "Hire me! The first thing we're going to do is get that money." And he said, "Oh no. I can't bug him for the money. He's my best client."

What? He's your best client? Who's your worst client?

Clients are not bad! Remember, if a client owes you ten or twenty thousand dollars, *you did that to yourself*. If I gave you a line of credit with no payment plan, no interest, no penalties, and no due date, you would take it. And if you're smart, you would use my free money instead of going to the bank.

Your customers are smart business people. Smart business people use money strategically. They use "free" money first, and they pay back expensive money first. So, if you're offering free money, you will be the first one they borrow from and the last one to be paid. And what happens when you finally ask for your money? Well, now they want to bargain. They'll pay ninety percent or eighty percent. Oops. Now you've just given a huge discount to people who have abused your kindness. Meanwhile, your good customers, who pay on time, still pay full price.

Remember: People don't value what they don't pay for. So, lesson number one is, don't give things away for free. Of course you might give a gift, or buy lunch for a client. But lesson number two is: Never give away your most important product or service. If you teach classes as a primary means of making money, never give away free classes. You might give away snippets or workbooks, but never the main product.

One time I thought I had a genius marketing idea. I went to my three best clients and said, "If you sign up for managed IT services at the new rate instead of the old rate, I will give you a brand-new desktop, $1,200 desktop," and they said, "Okay." Everybody took it, but none of them was particularly grateful.

One client literally never unboxed that desktop. In an office with fifteen employees, he didn't put it into use. It had no value to him. I didn't need to offer him that gift to get him to sign the deal. I should have bought him lunch instead—for a lot less money!

Okay. So, all equipment must be paid in advance.

And all subscription or monthly services should be paid in advance. And, as a side note, money owed to you is always worth less than face value.

Finally, let's look at *project labor*.

Project Labor Must Be Paid Fifty Percent Upfront

There are three major kinds of projects: Small, medium, and large. These can be sized by dollars or by time. A small project might take one hour of labor or one hundred and fifty dollars. A large project might take two hundred hours of labor or cost $30,000.

I really encourage you to get prepaid for at least half of what you expect a job to be. You have to determine what constitutes small and medium-sized jobs.

For larger, longer projects, you will probably have the milestone payments. But try to get prepaid for as much as you can. Some clients love to pre-pay so they can beat you up on price or get all kinds of freebies thrown in along the way. Some want to put the expense into a specific fiscal month or year.

A Few Rules about Getting Paid in Advance

There are only three simple rules you need to follow regarding getting paid up front:

- Manage the money carefully
- Avoid discounts
- Don't let clients make it an issue

Let me restate an important premise: This is business as usual. This is the way business is done. You're not doing clients a favor, and they're not doing you a favor. Getting prepaid for services is simply how business is done in the twenty-first century.

So, Rule #1 is that you must be good with managing money. Remember, that money might be in your bank, but it's not yours until the month you earn it. So, don't spend it all right away. Ideally, getting paid up front will be a purely positive experience and a blessing to your cash flow.

Pre-payments will start out as a nice cushion. Then they will grow to be a solid base, guaranteeing that employees are paid and the lights stay on. Eventually, they will simply be 90-100% of all the money you collect.

Rule #2 is to avoid discounts. Some clients are used to using money to gain leverage. They have the money to pay up front, so they use it as a way to get you to throw in a free month or some extra services. No.

Remember, they're not doing you a favor. They're just paying their bill. Remember the rule about discounts: Never discount the most important thing you sell. That obviously applies to your primary means of income!

Rule #3 is to avoid letting clients beat you up over pre-payment. Remember, there are people who use money strategically. The worst of these use money as a weapon. They beat you up for a discount, pay in advance, and they spend a year pushing the limits of your good will—because they're such good clients.

I had a client prepay a pretty good annual service contract and they proceeded to pay every invoice late. He would order equipment, fail to pay, and then complain when I asked. He said things like, "You've got $40,000 of my money."

And I'd say, "That was your choice. And it shouldn't keep you from paying your bill on time."

Remember, someone strategic like that has the money, and has some reason it's good for them to prepay. They really are not doing you a favor.

26. All After-Hours Work Is Billable

Let me give you two scenarios:

One: You ask me to work for you next Tuesday at four in the afternoon. This is mildly inconvenient for you. You will have to stop working for one hour. The charge is $150.

Two: You ask me to work for you next Tuesday at eight in the evening. This is very convenient for you. You will be at home, so you will not have to interrupt work in any way. The charge is $150.

You will choose Option Two, right? Think about the variables here: Your time, your convenience, my time, my convenience, your work, and the total cost.

In any analysis, you get more work done and are inconvenienced less if you have me work in the evening. Since the cost is the same, it would be silly of you to not inconvenience me. (Notice how I channeled my inner empath and used the word silly instead of stupid?)

Alright, let's take another stab at this.

Let's say I've created a great service plan based on a standard eight a.m. to five p.m. work day. You get X amount of labor within this plan each month. But notice, the plan does not include service next Tuesday evening!

If you want to increase your convenience and decrease mine, then you need to pay for that. Personally, I set this rate at twice the normal-hours rate. But at a minimum, you should charge the normal rate.

One other factor is involved here, which we have not addressed: I have a life! I work a full day on Tuesday, so I've already put in my time. Even if I "gave" you some free time, it would be my free time—literally.

Here's what I encourage service companies to do: Step back and look at the big picture. Remember the puzzle analogy. All of these rules fit together. If you want to grow your business, you need to adopt habits and policies that are scalable.

We're going to finish the book by looking at where your business fits into the "Bigger, Bigger Picture"—your life. Yes, you can work during the evening. Once in a while. Now and then. From time to time.

But remember that Success Is a Habit. It's hard to get into the habit of working in the evening and then try to get out of the habit of working in the evening.

Here's one of my favorite quotes from Horace Mann:

> **"Habit is a cable;**
> **we weave a thread of it each day,**
> **and at last we cannot break it."**

Aside from your family life and your personal life, there are some real business factors here. First, working all the time is unsustainable. So, second, don't build a business model based on unsustainable processes. Third, once you train clients that they can call you any time and you'll work for no extra charge, they will expect that. Moving to a more standard business model will be difficult.

Oh, and did you see what I just did there? Look around: The world works during business hours. With very few exceptions, you expect after-hours work to cost more, or not be available at all.

When was the last time you met with your doctor, lawyer, or stock broker at ten in the evening? Probably never, unless it's your friend.

You don't have to justify working normal business hours. You don't have to justify charging more for after-hours work. Don't have both sides of that conversation.

Many industries, including IT, perpetuate a myth that we are always available. People say things like, of course you have to work evenings and weekends.

But you don't. You really, really don't.

Here's what we did in my IT service companies. First, we set regular business hours. Second, our contract stated that all work outside normal business hours costs double.

In practical terms, that means that you need to be mindful about starting a job in the late afternoon. If it looks like you'll go past five o'clock, you talk to the client and ask them what they want to do.

"This job is covered until your service contract—until five o'clock. After five, I have to charge you twice the normal rate. Or I can wrap up for now and finish it at eight o'clock tomorrow morning. Then the labor is covered again." Ninety-nine percent of the time, the client's going to say, "Eight o'clock tomorrow is fine."

Remember, clients are like dogs. They'll do exactly what you train them to do.

And, as I mentioned in the last chapter, your clients are not taking advantage of you. You have set policies and they are following your policies. If you have a policy that charges the same (or nothing) to work evenings, then they have to assume that you know what you're doing. They will make a choice that inconveniences them least. When after-hours work costs more (or something), then they will choose to buy less of it. It's a simple, rational, business decision. And for you it's both sustainable and scalable.

27. It's Not Our Responsibility to Save the Client's Money

This is a quick one—but it's extremely important.

WAY too many people have a nagging feeling that they need to compete on price, even when there is zero factual evidence that it's true. (Don't get me wrong: If you're selling cheap socks and your store is across the street from Walmart, then you have to compete on price. But everyone else who's reading this probably doesn't.)

Keep these rules in mind:

- Branding is . . . everything you do
- The competition is irrelevant
- Don't have both sides of the conversation

Time and time again, I talk to business owners who sell what I consider to be second- or third-rate materials. They sell refurbished equipment or used equipment.

Don't get me wrong. If your business is used stuff, that's fine. That's your brand.

But if your brand is more on the "professional" side, then you need to sell professional-quality stuff. There are lots of pricing strategies around good-better-best. But in most service industries, the options are not laid out that way.

Let's say that I ask you for a quote on a job. What will it cost me to . . . ? What I *do not want* is for you to bring me three fully fleshed-out service quotes. That's too much information!

And never forget: Your client does not know as much about all this stuff as you do. If they did, you wouldn't have a business. So, whether you're quoting a job to paint a house, build a store front in the cloud, or update the lighting fixtures in an office building, you *always* know more than the client!

Why does that matter? For one simple reason: If a client asks you for a quote and then does not buy, it's your fault! Period. It just is. They came to you with a simple request: "Give me a good reason to give you a bunch of money." But you didn't give them a good reason.

There are two important things to remember in this situation:

First,

> **"There's no such thing as a confused buyer.**
> **If they're confused, they're not buying."**

I first heard that from my friend Patrick Schwerdtfeger (see *Webify Your Business, Internet Marketing Secrets for the Self-Employed*).

Second, when the only thing a client understands is price, then the cheapest price is often their only option.

If you confuse your prospect with options, then you're likely to get the question, "What would you do?" But, if you're the kind of person who gives three options when the client asks one question, then you are also likely to be the kind of person who hems and haws.

That means that you feel silly (see previous chapter) endorsing the most expensive option. But you know the cheapest option is a really bad idea. So you proceed through a litany of the good, bad, and ugly of each option. Now you're doing mental gymnastics about return on investment, warranties, and relevant productivity.

Did you ever see the Far Side cartoon about what we say to dogs and what they hear? I'll give you a clue. What the dog hears is "Blah blah Ginger blah blah blah . . . Ginger blah blah."

Ginger doesn't actually understand your language.

Neither does your client.

I know you've been through this with a doctor. I have, more than once. Doctors love to give you options without advice.

Let's say you have a swollen nerve in your foot. We can stick a needle into it with cortisone. We have to mix the cortisone with lidocaine because it's so painful that you're going to cry. We only have to do that every three to six months until it no longer solves the problem.

OR we can give you a series of seven or eight shots of alcohol in the bottom of your foot, once a week for seven or eight weeks. If we're lucky, that will shrink the nerve. And it's not very invasive. Still, lots of pain.

OR we can cut open your foot, dig around, and take out as much of the swollen nerve as we can find, then sew you up. If we're lucky, there will be a lot less pain once the swelling goes down. We'll try to go in through the top of your foot to avoid a scar on the bottom of your foot.

Yikes! "What would you do, doc?"

"Well, it's not my decision."

Unlike a medical procedure, most services you sell have a very clear option: Do nothing. Or, at least, do nothing now. Ignore it. Pretend the problem isn't there.

If you confuse your client with options, you will make fewer sales. This is a simple truth.

Now, let's go back to the question of knowledge. Why are you even tempted to go down the road of giving options? It is probably because you feel you should be saving the client money—or at least making it an option.

Take a minute. Look around your client's parking lot. Or just see which car they drove to this meeting. Chances are very good that your client has money to spend on things that they see as bringing value.

I've had a number of clients who actually *ask* for the best. They won't buy the i7 processor if the i9 will be out within a year. They want the latest generation. It's not even that they want to look cool with the latest. They just believe that the highest value they can get is to buy the best available at the time.

I remember one client who really needed a kind of technology that he'd never heard of (a power switch that could be controlled over the Internet). I explained it to him and even gave him a demo unit. He honestly needed the lowest possible functionality for this.

But that's not who he was! He proceeded to ask about additional options, sizes, functionality, warranties, and more. He was basically trying to get enough information to buy the absolute best remote power switch on the market. He literally spent twenty times more than he needed to. And he was happy. Even if "good" would do the job.

I had a different client who was a heart surgeon with five other heart surgeons on his staff. We helped them build an amazing set of technologies that allowed them to share video heart images with doctors in other cities and do remote consultations.

This doctor did not ask for the "best" of everything. All he asked for was 100% uptime. The income per minute in his office was completely reliant on technology. Downtime was too expensive to contemplate. It was literally intolerable.

The worst thing that could possibly happen with this doctor was downtime. And when he asked the question, "Why did this break?"

the worst possible answer would be: "Because I was trying to save you some money."

Saving money is *one* motivation for your clients. But it is absolutely not the only one.

But, again, over-quoting is your enemy.

You see, even when saving money is not the primary motivator, you can force a client to make a decision based on money. Ironically, this comes from giving them too many options and too much information.

Let's go back to that request for a quote. In the discussion above, you gave the client three options with lots of details. Again, let's assume the client is overwhelmed with information they don't really understand. But, this time, the client must make a decision. They can't opt out.

When the client tries to boil down your options, here's what they see:

Good	**Better**	**Best**
Blah blah blah	Blah blah blah	Blah blah blah
Low Price	Mid Price	High Price

Admit it: If this is all you understood, you'd probably choose the cheapest option as well. A small group of clients will pick the middle because, in absence of other information, they avoid the bottom and top of the market. A smaller group will pick the most expensive because that's just how they roll.

But most clients will make the decision on price.

Notice that I said in the absence of other information? I kind of slid that in there. You gave them lots of information. In fact, an overwhelming amount. And that's really the same thing, if they're not in your industry and not an enthusiast who just happens to study this stuff on the side.

In other words: You pretty much forced them to make the wrong decision.

Recommend the Best; Give Alternatives If Asked

The simple solution to this problem is: Start with the "doctor" question. If this was your business, what would you do? That's really just a way of asking, what's the right solution or what's the best solution?

Quote the best. Yes, it might be expensive. But you'll be amazed at how many people say yes. After all, they didn't ask you to give them homework. They asked you to give them a quote to fix a problem. If the client says that it's way outside their price range, or they ask if there are lower-priced alternatives, then you can begin discussing options. Now you're in a two-way conversation that is focused on finding the right value for the client.

Now you can talk about some details. You can educate the client. They don't need, or want, to know everything. But if *this* part could be cheaper or *that* phase could be delayed until next year, then we can move forward.

As a side note, I highly discourage you from starting at the bottom. You've seen this on Internet forums. "Does anyone know of a free software I can use to run a hospital that's 100% guaranteed HIPAA compliant and meets all the federal requirements for grants?"

Or, the alternative. Someone will ask for the best *something* out there, and half the answers are for junky solutions that you can try for free.

Many people assume that everyone is trying to save money first.

That's simply not true. If you believe that, you need to consider hanging out with a different crowd.

It costs money to be in business.

When people start out at the bottom, selling used junk and refurbished equipment, I find that they limit their company's ability to excel.

Remember, the way you do anything is the way you do everything. It's really hard to build a business on people who are super cheap, rely on second-hand junk, and expect you to keep replacing it again and again. Eventually, you'll realize that you want your company to be very profitable and to throw off some cash from time to time, so you can retire one day.

When you decide that you need to focus on clients who can afford to spend enough money to keep you in business, it will be like starting over. None of your old clients will fit your new business model. And very few will be easily converted.

And worst of all, you'll notice that clients leave you as soon as they can afford someone else. Why? You're the cheap one who peddles the lowest end solution. You're not going to be the one who brings value-based solutions.

Remember, back in Chapter 4, when we talk about The [YOUR] Way of doing business? What is your way? I hope it's **Recommend the Best; Give Alternatives If Asked.**

28. You Don't Have to Pick up Every Nickel You Find

This rule is different from "You're not responsible for every lost dog that shows up on your doorstep."

This rule is about escaping the "poverty" mentality that you simply must take every job and every dollar that's offered. That's really, honestly, not true.

But here's the really weird reality of this rule: The misconception that you have to take every job you can will not keep your company small. But it will keep your company unprofitable.

I've seen very small and very large companies that believe they have to pick up every nickel they find. But I've never seen a prosperous, profitable company that believes it.

Not everything that looks like an opportunity is really an opportunity. There are clients who will only buy a couple of hours here and a couple of hours there. If you let them, they will stick around at the bottom of your list. Eventually, they will turn into clients that you have to get rid of one day.

Note: This is one of my primary examples of why these rules are "absolutely unbreakable." This rule applies even in the post-COVID economic recession. This rule applies when the economy is growing exponentially or shrinking fast.

This rule is true when you're just starting out, when you're well established, and even when your business makes mistakes and you find yourself rebuilding your client base.

Every once in a while, someone will argue with me (usually on an

Internet forum) and call out this advice. They say things like, "Karl doesn't understand what it's like. Sometimes you just have to take every job you can."

Not true. I *do* understand. I've started out. I've re-started. I've lost large clients. I've been through more than one major recession. I've built three businesses now that started with just me and no other employees.

I do understand.

I put this chapter in the "Billing and Finance" section because I want you to look back on lots of earlier chapters about clients, branding, priorities, and, of course, finances. You cannot simply go do "anything" and call it a business. If you want your business to be around in five or ten years, you have to build it intentionally.

Remember: Nothing happens by itself.

Just because you want to do whatever you do, that doesn't make it a business. A business has a reason for existing. If all you want is to "do" your trade and get money in exchange, that's called a job. Go get a job. But if you want to be in business, you owe your customer more than just trading dollars for hours.

There are probably hundreds of people who cut hair near where you live. Why do you go to your favorite? Is it price? Quality? Speed? A nice atmosphere? Location? Whatever it is, it's *something*. And that something was created by the owner. He or she put the business at that location, picked out the furnishings, created the atmosphere, set the pricing, and so forth.

In other words, they created the business. They didn't just hang out on the sidewalk and whisper, "Hey buddy. Wanna haircut?" to everyone who walked by.

In my opinion, most people who think they need to take every little job they're offered have no plan. Their business has no reason to exist. They don't fill a gap. The business has no purpose. It has no self-awareness.

Some people start with that attitude and never lose it—even after they have moved way beyond that reality. I've seen companies with millions of dollars in sales who still don't turn down any prospective clients.

And here's the absolute truth: Every company I've seen like that is unprofitable. Yes, they have five million dollars on their top line (revenue), but nothing on the bottom line (profit).

A company that tries to serve everyone, no matter what, ends up under-serving their most important clients in order to over-serve clients who don't deserve it. And why don't they deserve it? Primarily because those clients are so focused on saving money that they will leave you in a minute.

Why would you reschedule a client that has signed a contract so you can help somebody who just wants to give you a few hours of labor? You don't need to do that. Don't have that mentality of poverty.

When a client is willing to make a commitment to you, you should make a commitment to them. I would much rather give a free hour to my best client than to sell an hour to somebody I'm never going to see again. I think the time is better spent trying to please the client that is a known good client.

Remember the rule, "Every client is on a service agreement." Ask the fly-by-night client if they'll sign an agreement.

Money and "Fit"

Run a QuickBooks report on Sales / by Client / Labor / Summary for the last twelve whole months. Add a column for "column percent" and then sort from high to low.

Obviously, I encourage you to be good at tracking labor. Now look at the labor involved in the bottom 20% of that report. It's amazing how much time tiny little clients take. And you just don't need that money. There are other ways to make money.

Remember: Clients have to bring a certain minimal amount of labor (money) in order to be on your customer list. Do your own math and figure it out. If every customer was this size, could you make a living?

If clients are below the minimum size required to make your business viable, then you don't have a business. You have headaches and stress, but you don't have profit.

Aside from money, you also need clients who are a good fit for your business mode. For example, a customer who is super-needy is probably not very profitable. In coaching, when we analyze the profitability of clients, we almost always find that the largest clients are the least profitable.

The biggest client that we ever fired was paying us almost exactly $150,000 per year. That was about $75K in hardware and software and $75K in labor. But they were unmanageable.

I literally had these visions in my head that the boss would run up and down the aisles of his own company with a beehive in one hand and a baseball bat in the other, just beating it as much as he could. He would blow up our phones and then blow up all of our cell phones and then open seventeen tickets and then send emails to everybody, and there would literally be thirty tickets in the system in a matter of five minutes.

One day my brother (who was the president of that company at the time) came to me and said, "How much of my salary will it take for you to fire these guys and never do business with them again?" And we sat down and we calculated it because we keep track of everything in our CRM (customer relationship management system) and in QuickBooks.

We calculated that the profit from this client was about $27,000. And we realized, we don't have to replace the $150,000 in income; we just have to replace the $27,000 in profit. So, we got rid of them and the stress in our company was dramatically reduced. We sold all that time serving clients who appreciated us more.

"Fit" also matters when you think about your company mission and vision. Does the so-called opportunity in front of you fit with where you want to go and what you want your company to be? If not, then it's not a real opportunity.

As I'm writing this chapter, I had a conversation with a friend who is starting a new business. He's been at it for about six months. I was talking to him about a ten thousand dollar opportunity—and he quoted this rule back to me: "You know how you always say you don't have to pick up every nickel? Ten thousand dollars would be nice, but that's not really the work I want to be doing." He then went on to describe the revenue stream that he *did* want to build.

When your business exists for a purpose—and it should—you can say no to money that doesn't align with the longer-term vision. Another way to say that is: If you don't have a vision, then the purpose of your business is to scrounge around and pick up spare change.

Summary:

1. Don't argue with me on this
2. It doesn't matter whether you're starting out or very large, the rule still applies
3. It doesn't matter what the economy is doing, the rule still applies

You don't have to pick up every nickel you find.

29. If A Client Has A Past-Due Balance, Their Service Is Cut Off

This is another quickie. It falls into the category of things you will learn eventually. The sooner you learn it, the better off you'll be.

Back in Chapter 25, I mentioned business owners I've worked with who were owed lots of money. In one case, $70,000 from a single client. Getting prepaid for everything is one way to prevent that.

Another way is to cut off service.

Note: Depending on your business, it may be completely impractical to cut off service. For example, in the IT industry, I'm not going to start by shutting down the Internet, stopping all email, and killing the point of sale terminals. But you have to do *something*.

Even if you try to get prepaid for everything, there's always something that gets billed. Whether that piece is small or large, it *does* need to be paid. As with many, many things, you train your clients on how to treat you. So if you train them to pay late (or not at all), that's your fault.

I think many small business owners get side tracked into believing that the "right" way to do everything is with the good old handshake. "You don't ask a client to sign a contract!"

And that quaint nineteenth century view of the world gets them into trouble. As I mentioned before, your clients don't see themselves as taking advantage of you. But if they owe money to the landlord, the bank, the electric company, their suppliers, and you, then you're just another person with your hand out.

Let's say that you're a little short on cash this month. Who would you pay first? Well, it depends on who is the most persistent, and who is the most forgiving. You might win over the electric company for one month, but not two.

The point is: If you charge late fees, and interest, then you move your invoices up the hierarchy. If you threaten to cut off services (whatever that means), then you move way up the hierarchy.

And please don't worry about irritating or losing clients. First, clients who owe you money need to be gradually removed from your client list anyway. Second, don't have both sides of the conversation. In other words: Talk to your client! Hold a roadmap meeting. Figure out what's going on and what the plan is.

But part of the plan has to be that you get paid!

Third, you probably won't lose a client no matter how bad things get. I know that sounds unbelievable to some of you. But it's true.

Remember that discussion at the end of Chapter 25 about clients abusing your good will because they prepaid for services. I had a long relationship with one of those clients. It started out with him prepaying one service for a year, and then proceeding to pay everything else late for many months.

Eventually, I sent him a note and told him that we were suspending his services. What it really meant was that he could enter service tickets, but we wouldn't do any new work for him.

You could hear him cussing me out 150 miles away. But he paid his bill. Then he proceeded to complain about every bill for months. We cut off his service about once a month for almost six months. Eventually, he learned that everything went a lot smoother when he just paid us on time.

Now this part might surprise you. First, that was a big client for us. In all, he spent about $60,000 per year with us. But, you see, it's not about the amount of money that needs to be paid: The fact is, the money needs to be paid!

Second, that troublesome start to a relationship resulted in him continuing as our client for about seven years. He was still a client when I sold my company. And he'd paid his bills on time for six of those years.

Third, he remained a client of the company after I sold it, but he went back to not paying bills on time. The new owner had to go through the entire "training" process again. It turns out, he just likes to pay late. I don't know if he thinks he saves money that way or what.

But the bottom line is: His decision to work with us was separate from his decision about how and when to pay. As demonstrated by beating us up on the prepayment the first year, he is simply one of those business owners that uses money strategically—and not always nicely.

And here's the end of the story. Nine years after I sold that business, I was still managing this guy's domain names. I sent a note asking whether he wanted them renewed. He sent back a kind memo about how he was selling the business, but he really appreciated everything we'd done for them over the years. He told me to say goodbye to any technicians I was still in contact with, and he wished me well in all future endeavors.

Remember the rule, "We only work with people we like?" Well, keep in mind that even friends have disagreements sometimes. That doesn't mean you give up and quit. But it also doesn't mean that you let them abuse your good will.

I told that story because I want to believe that you won't lose clients just because you have the same business practices as all the other successful businesses your clients work with.

"Cutting off service" can be as simple as saying that you can't call us except in the case of emergencies. I know that doesn't sound like a big threat to you, but your clients rely on you. And that means they want access—even if they rarely need it.

This advice comes at the end of the finance section because it's the final tool you need to keep your finances under control.

Section VII
Rules for IT Service Providers and MSPs

30. There's No Such Thing as "All You Can Eat"

31. Only Sell and Recommend Business-Class Equipment

32. Replace All Hardware at The End of the Warranty

33. Technicians must work in real time

34. Use a TSR Log

35. Use a PSA (Professional Services Automation) Tool

30. There's No Such Thing as "All You Can Eat"

**"Managed Service consists of the
maintenance of the operating system and software"**

First, a story (a true story).

Many years ago, I bought a brand-new car. And there was a tire dealership just one block from where I parked. It was one of those places that promised absolutely top-shelf service. In fact, they made a point of saying that I could trust all my warranty work to them.

So, I took my car there – for everything. I told the mechanic that I'm putting my new car in his hands. I went there for oil changes, alignments, scheduled service, etc. Everything.

Then one day, after about two years, they told me that I needed new tires. What? I don't drive that much. How could I need new tires?

The mechanic explained: It looks like these tires have never been rotated.

WHAT?!!?

How is that possible, I wanted to know. I took my car in to their shop exclusively. They did all the work. They adjusted the breaks. They did the inspections. They did everything.

And – more importantly – I was a great customer. I didn't complain. I didn't resist. I spent every penny they asked me to spend and I had them perform every bit of maintenance they recommended.

Why have you never rotated my tires?

"You never asked us to."

Period.

I explained how much I had trusted them, and put my car in their loving hands. They should understand why I expected them to take care of all the details. But they did *not* understand. Was I wrong here? Was I expecting too much?

Yes, I was wrong. Yes, I expected too much.

For the record: It's too bad that you can't turn over your car to someone and have them just fix everything, and do perfect preventive maintenance.

I was trying to buy something they didn't sell. I had made assumptions about how much of my maintenance could be turned over to someone else. And, it turns out, it's less than "everything." (For the record, I still find this odd since the car comes with a book that lists every single piece of maintenance that needs to be done – including rotating the tires.)

But there's still a limit to how much maintenance you can turn over to someone else. Sadly for me, there was no "managed service" equivalent in the world of automotive maintenance.

It's important to remember this. The customer's assumptions and the service providers assumptions may be very different. Clients want to delegate as much responsibility to you as possible, for a reasonable fee. But, of course, there are also assumptions about what is reasonable.

There is always a line between what's included and what's not. Period. This is simply one of the truths of the universe. It's true in all businesses at all levels. A corollary of that truth is that the client will always assume that more is included than what the service provider thinks is included.

Before I became a consultant, I managed all the technology for computer systems in the company I worked for. It was a vast and dizzying array of old and new, large and small. We had HP 3000 mini computers, Microsoft servers, Novell systems, fax servers, banks of modems, multi-state Internet connections, five different backup systems. It was a big, confusing conglomeration. But one thing was clear: Whether directly or indirectly, I was responsible for all of it.

When I went out on my own and became a consultant, I assumed the same responsibility. I told clients that I would be responsible for everything, if they turned it over to me. I asked them not to make changes, not to buy new equipment, and forbid other vendors from touching anything without my knowledge.

It was years later that I discovered that almost no one provides this kind of service when they start out. Many learn hard lessons along the way and end up providing comprehensive service, but few start that way.

I take pride in being one of the early pioneers of managed services. And for me, it will always be a maintenance-focused service offering. Managed service does not require a flat fee, monthly billing, an RMM, or a PSA. But it *does* require preventive maintenance as *the* key component.

Managed service is an IT service delivery model that requires a certain balance of goals in order to be successful. These goals include:

- Provide extremely reliable IT services
- Focus on preventive maintenance

And, ideally, it will include:

- Emphasis on flat-fee services (flat fee is not "all you can eat")
- Use modern tools to deliver services
- Use modern tools to manage internal processes and procedures
- Get paid in advance for as much as possible

The benefits of this model are numerous:.

- Clients enjoy more computer/service "uptime"
- Clients appreciate predictable, flattened billing
- IT service providers enjoy predictable recurring revenue
- Service providers can manage more clients (endpoints) with fewer staff
- Service providers become more professional
- And, of course, IT service providers become more profitable *when they do it right*

That last bit is very important: When they do it right. Many people have mistaken "managed services" for flat fee billing. Flat fee is an invoicing decision, not a business model. And those who make this mistake are likely to make the biggest mistake of all: They offer all-you-can-eat pricing or AYCE.

There is no such thing as AYCE. Anyone who says that's what they're offering is either lying to you or lying to themselves. There are always limits. All the client can eat is all of your profit. I won't repeat the whole rant here, but I have lots of rants against AYCE in my blog posts, videos, and books.

Here my only point is to demonstrate how bad you can go wrong when you get the wrong mix of guiding rules.

Whenever someone tells me that they're not making money with an IT service business, or making less than before, I know for a fact that they are doing it wrong. Whatever the problem is, you should be making money when your hourly rate is given in hundreds of dollars. Most of the time, people who are losing money in this business are giving away too much labor for not enough money.

Remember the quote at the top of this chapter: Managed service consists of the maintenance of the software and operating system.

When you look at the balance of things that make managed services work, it is a bit complicated. You have to have a commitment to preventive maintenance. If your service is not focused on maintenance first, it will be hard to move clients over to a flat fee model. Business models are based on value propositions. You have to get the client hooked on the value of preventive maintenance before you can move them to maintenance for a flat fee.

Another un-balancing mistake is to avoid using RMM tools (remote monitoring and management). My managed service was originally based on the price of delivering all the services manually. But additional profit comes from automating that service. For example, manual monthly server maintenance might take about an hour and a half. But with RMM, it might be reduced to fifteen minutes (to verify a restore from backup).

When MSPs (managed service providers) fail to adopt good tools, they are less likely to focus on preventive maintenance or automated maintenance. As a result, they earn less money. They also see less value from the managed service model. If you don't start with preventive maintenance, it's hard to make this model work. It's also harder to sell.

In fact, many so-called MSPs have made the ultimate mistake of never providing the preventive maintenance at all (paid or included in the fee). As a result, they have to wait until something breaks and then go fix it. That is exactly opposite to the managed service model. It is break/fix tech support – even if they've managed to sell it for a flat fee.

I have made the argument over the last several years that many people who call themselves managed service providers are not actually providing managed services. They have mistaken the invoicing model for the value-based business model.

Thinking About Your Business

Another truly great book you should read, if you haven't already, is *The E-Myth Revisited* by Michael Gerber. One of the key messages of that book is that you have to take time to work ON your business, rather than just working IN the business.

If you just work *in* the business, you are likely to look around, see what others are doing, and copy it. After all, you're too busy working in the day-to-day world to figure out business models and worry about the philosophy of your business.

But if you want to be successful, you must take time to work *on* the business. From Simon Sinek's question of *Why* to the smallest detail of daily processes and procedures, you have to create your business with intention. If you don't spend time on this, you will have a business that has no purpose and cannot help you fulfill your personal or professional goals.

So, you need to allocate time to regularly work on your business. Work on the why. Work on the how. Think about what service delivery should look like. Think about the clients and employees you want to attract. Think about the company you want to work in – and take pride in – five years down the road.

Once you have a (somewhat) grand vision of what you want your company to be and where you want it to take you, ask this question: What are the chances that your vision will come into existence by chance? You have to admit it: The chance is zero.

My personal and business motto is: **Nothing Happens by Itself**.

Imagine that you own a lumberyard and it gets hit by a huge windstorm. Lumber and windows and nails fly everywhere. Now imagine that the wind stops and you find a fully constructed four-bedroom home where your lumberyard used to be. What are the chances of that? Zero.

It's the same with your business. If you spend all your time taking care of the daily chores – stacking lumber – then only one thing can result from the winds of business that will hit your company over the next five years. It will be a scattered mess and you'll spend lots of time re-stacking things.

If you want the big, beautiful house, you need to make it happen. You need to lay down a foundation, begin building the framework, and bring your dream into existence. It might be more work than you imagined. It might take longer. And it might end up being just two bedrooms. But you will build it if you choose to.

It won't build itself.

And no one else will build it for you.

Managed Service is not a big, complicated business model. It is surprisingly simple to understand and explain. But that doesn't mean it's easy to execute. You have to buy into some specific beliefs (e.g., You'll be more profitable if everyone pays in advance). And you have to make all the pieces work together.

You have to have mantras to help yourself (and everyone who works with you) remember all the pieces that make up this puzzle of awesome service delivery and profit. New employees won't get it. Until they suddenly do. Clients may not get it. Until they suddenly do. You need to be an evangelist for your business model.

That requires you to spend time working *on* your business and thinking *about* your business.

This book is all about the "absolutely unbreakable rules" of service delivery that I've come up with over the years to help me evangelize to my employees, my clients, my vendors, and the rest of the IT Community.

If you're in IT service delivery, I think you'll find these rules to be about a 95% fit with your business.

But never forget where about the automobile maintenance example: You have to make sure you and the client have a clear understanding of what is – and is not – included in managed service. Every disagreement on this will boil down to a disagreement on assumptions.

You eliminate assumptions by being very clear about what's included for a flat fee, what's included for an extra fee, and what's not included at all. And then you need to make sure you deliver at least as much as what you promise!

31. Only Sell and Recommend Business-Class Equipment

One of the most common discussions I see on various online forums is about firewalls. And within that topic there seems to be a never-ending discussion about getting clients to use a "real" firewall versus the one provided by the ISP or some low-end piece of junk they found at the office supply store.

Whether it's firewalls, servers, switches, printers, network access points, desktop machines, laptops, or anything else, there's an amazing variety of things that you could sell in this business. I encourage you to *only quote the best* stuff and only sell something else if a client asks you to.

Remember "don't have both sides of that conversation." One time I had a conversation where a client said, "Why did this break?" and I had to say, "We were trying to save you money," and he literally said the words to me, "I didn't ask you to save me money."

Boom.

I'll never forget that: I didn't ask you to save me money.

Obviously, his technology was more important than his money. He has enough money, apparently. But just as there are people who drive old Ford Fiestas and there are people who drive new BMWs, everybody gets to choose which car they drive. Everybody gets to choose the level at which they want their network to operate. If you only sell the good stuff, if you only quote good firewalls, brand names with all of the goodies attached, most of your clients are going to take your advice. And when they have one experience that tests that, then they will be sold on it.

I remember one time, I had a client that always bought what I told them to buy, even though they thought I was a little expensive. I only sold business-class HP desktops and HP servers. One reason for that is that I have experienced only two hard drive failures in thirty years. Well, one of those happened at this client. Actually, it *almost* happened. On boot-up the HP reported that a drive was about to fail.

Of course, it was under warranty. I called tech support, and that afternoon someone came to the client's office, put in a new hard drive, and imaged over the data. The client literally said the words to me, "I always wondered whether we were making the right decision to buy these desktops that you recommend and now I know that we made the right decision."

That's what you want the client to hear, not, "Why is this piece of junk failing again?" "Oh, because I saved you $200 on a desktop." Remember: the purchase price of a desktop computer is about one-fourth of the total cost over three years. So don't try to save $200 and end up costing the client more.

So, quote the good stuff and sell the good stuff. If a client balks and says they really can't afford it, then you can quote the lower-cost option. But start with the right choice first! Remember: It's not your job to save the client money. And don't have both sides of the conversation.

I'm a big believer that everybody should have a line card for the hardware, software, and services you sell. This is particularly important with hardware. The line card is simply a list of the preferred one or two brands that you sell. This is good to have, even if you're the only salesperson.

For example, with printers, you can say, "We sell HP and we sell Brother. We don't sell Epson." There are so many kinds of printers you could be selling. Please don't try to sell every kind of printer offered by Ingram, D&H, Tech Data, etc.

Why not sell "everything" you can? Very simply, you can get to know the ins and outs of two brands. Your sales people and your technicians can learn these two brands backwards and forwards. You'll know what to sell into a workgroup, into a small company, or into a specific department.

There's a right printer for everything. You cannot start out you quoting process by getting a list of every printer for sale at every distributor. It will easily overwhelm you. Instead, focus on a couple of brands for each item you sell.

Pick one primary brand for servers, and maybe an alternative. Do the same for desktop and laptop computers. Pick one primary brand and a backup brand for monitors, routers, switches, UPSs, speakers, and so forth. For each brand, you will learn the lines that are good, better, and best. Quote the best, and then when clients push back you can go with something else.

When you focus on a limited number of brands, your sales people will become more effective and more well-informed. They can't learn everything, so don't ask them to try. Similarly, your technicians will learn all the quirks and undocumented features for one or two brands. They can dig much deeper into the knowledge of a few brands that they could with "all" brands.

And remember, ignore your competition. Even if your competition is Staples, do not base your prices on what you clients would pay if they bought equipment themselves. I have always sold my hardware at cost plus 25% and it's frequently more expensive than going to Best Buy, Staples, Amazon, CDW, or anybody else. But I tell my clients, "I'm selling you the right thing."

One time, I had a client who tried to save money. He looked at the quote, got the model number, and bought a desktop PC that had the same model number. But, somehow, he managed to buy a machine with zero level 2 cache. He complained to me, "This is the slowest machine I've ever seen in my life. You were going to sell me this piece of junk."

And I said, "No, I was not. I don't even know where you found a machine with zero level 2 cache, but I would not have sold you that. I would have sold you the right thing, which is why it costs more." He wanted to save that money and ended up just frustrating himself.

Building the Perfect Network

There are a handful of elements that go into building the perfect network. (Perfect means that nothing ever breaks.) These include:

- Business class hardware
- . . . that's less than three years old, so still under warranty
- The newest generation of operating system, unless it revved in the last three years
- The newest generation of software
- All hardware, software, and operating systems are patched and up to date

If you sell people only the good stuff, you will have less maintenance to do. If you require that everything is under warranty, things won't break as much. Imagine a network where everything is three years old or less, everything is patched, fixed, updated, and maintained all the time. Essentially, nothing breaks. You get to collect your managed service fee but you don't have to actually put out much labor.

Managed service is like an HMO. You get all your money on the first day of the month. You only have to spend money when something breaks, so it's in your best interest that nothing ever breaks. When you limit your product offering, that also helps your service team because they only have to know a handful of product lines. And so forth.

And one final note: The only way you can start to get good pricing with some brands is to sell enough volume to earn better pricing. Sticking to one primary brand and one secondary brand will help a lot.

Used and Refurbished Hardware

No.

Just no.

Please do not be tempted to sell used or refurbished equipment – unless you're in the used equipment business.

If you're in the business described above, and you are pushing clients to rely on new equipment that's still under warranty, then the world of used/refurbished pulls you in the wrong direction. The fact is, old stuff breaks more. It just does.

If you focus on a business model that relies on uptime preventive maintenance, it is simply a fact that old, used, and even refurbished equipment will require more maintenance. If you've been in the business long enough, you've bought a "cheap" brand name drive that is warrantied for thirty days, breaks down immediately after that, and there's no support from the manufacturer.

Even if a refurbished piece of equipment is 90% as reliable as new, *that's a lot less reliable* than new! It is a false economy to believe that you have saved money with such equipment.

And if you buy into the flat-fee billing model, then used equipment is virtually guaranteed to lower your profit margin, due to this increased need for support labor.

On a related note, we always made sure that equipment taken out of service was marked as "bad" or "used." And, in the case of questionable cables or adapters, we cut them in half or physically broke them so they cannot be put back into service. There are few things that will waste your time better than tracking down an intermittent connection due to a cable that was put back into service by a cheap client!

I know many technicians who have piles of *old* stuff filling their shelves. After all, an 80 GB hard drive might be perfectly serviceable. It works, in some sense. It's useless by today's standards, but it works. I know I find it hard to throw away a 250 GB hard drive. But I also have absolutely no use for it. I'm not putting it into a server, a desktop, or even a laptop. Whatever's in those machines now is guaranteed to be larger than that.

We make a habit of moving all old equipment to the recycle pile immediately. If technicians want to take something home, for their own use, that's fine. Everything else goes to the recycler as soon as possible.

I know I get preachy sometimes. But few rules have made more money for my companies over the years than this one: Sell business class equipment, intended to be in service for three years, and sell it with a three-year warranty. And not far behind that is: Don't sell used or refurbished equipment. You're guaranteed to see it again!

32. Replace All Hardware at The End of the Warranty

I hinted at this in the last chapter. Part of the perfect network is business class equipment. I use that term to define equipment that is intended for intense daily usage, and most of the time that means it comes with a three-year warranty. We push clients very strongly on this.

All equipment needs to be maintained. Old equipment needs to be maintained more. And maintaining old equipment costs more money. And there's a natural *downhill* slide. Eventually, hardware cannot be patched enough to be safe from new malware attacks. It becomes permanently unsafe.

In addition, old hardware cannot take advantage of new operating system functions. First one thing, then another. Eventually, it's just not very functional by modern standards.

And, finally, old hardware becomes too dated to take on new hardware peripherals. Today it's the new video card standard. Next, it's the latest version of USB or Wi-Fi. Again, it just becomes less functional by today's standards.

It's an odd but natural human reaction: We don't see the money we pour into old equipment. Whether it's a ten-year-old car, a ten-year-old refrigerator, or a five-year-old phone, old stuff just costs more to operate.

This is particularly true of anything that clients use to make money in their business. Older stuff is slow, often insecure or dangerous, and has higher repair bills than newer stuff.

One way to educate clients on this is your monthly newsletter (I hope you have a monthly newsletter). That's a great place to start the mantra, and repeat it as often as you can: "As you know, we like to encourage people to replace their equipment every three years. So, replace some of it each year. The goal is to make sure everything's always going to be under warranty."

You can repeat that advice at every opportunity. Repeat it when you're talking to clients.

For us, this is three years. And so, we encourage clients to replace one-third of their desktops and laptops every year. That way, the cost is evened out, and everything in their office is always under warranty! You might choose four years, but you need to get four years of warranty coverage.

I also love to do cost projections that are one month longer than the warranty. So, for example, if equipment has a three-year warranty, I do a 37-month projection. Let's say that equipment costs $10,000. "Here is your cost on day one. $10,000. And here's the maintenance for 36 months. And, finally, here's the 37th month – when you'll need to buy that equipment again."

Clients are happy to see this, even though it looks expensive, because it gives them some idea of what it costs in the long run.

Note: If you sell business class equipment, as described in the last chapter, then you may be able to get away with an extended warranty. You should sell such warranties! You should also help the client to get financing and to balance out those costs over the life of the equipment.

It's also a natural human tendency to think about transactions as if they are a one-time activity, even if we know they're not. If you buy an air conditioner with a ten-year warranty, do you calculate the cost of repairs and maintenance after that? Probably not. Most people don't. But a ten-year-old, out-of-warranty AC unit burns electricity much faster than a newer unit. Period. It just does.

We all know that new things, under warranty, don't break. At least 99% of the time. And if you sell quality equipment, it should be absolutely 100% trouble-free for at least the life of the warranty. But if the client keeps it for an additional five years, six years, etc., there will be a point at which you can guarantee that it's *going* to have problems.

In the computer world, an eight-year-old server (or laptop or desktop computer) is a piece of junk. It just is. There's no non-piece-of-junk at that age.

What's the ideal age of equipment in your industry? Talk to your clients about that number! Make it a known quantity.

Whatever your specialty, I'm sure you can imagine the "perfect" client setup. All the equipment is under warranty. Repairs are cheap, covered, or non-existent. Everything just works all the time. This is possible. And it's a great model for the vision your clients should have about how thing *could be*.

I know lots of clients are penny-pinchers. But don't fall into the trap of projecting that on all your other clients. Lots of people are not penny-pinchers. Focus on people who can actually afford your service. It will make life a lot easier.

Examples for Your Clients

Here are two of my favorite examples, which clients can relate to. First: Servers. Aside from the fact that "the cloud" is a real thing and they probably don't need a server . . .

A four-year-old server is probably the slowest machine in the office. As network cards go faster, you have gradually upgraded all the machines in the office to draw more and more data from the server. In addition, the memory and processor speeds on all the desktop PCs have grown faster and faster. In the meantime, the server that was cutting-edge four years ago is now two generations behind everything in the office.

Note: You may be able to bolster this argument if you have a server with 100-mb network cards while desktops have gigabit cards. Or, similarly, if the Internet connection now exceeds the maximum speed of the server NICs.

Second: Firewalls (and, to a lesser extent, routers).

The number of mathematical calculations required by a firewall is staggering – and grows all the time. First, the speed of the connection takes a big jump. If you have a 250 mbps Internet connection, you need to have an external port that's at least that fast. If you have a 100 mb network port on the outside of the firewall, then your Internet speed will never exceed 100 mb. Period.

On top of that, firewalls need to do a lot more than move packets. A firewall needs to open every packet and make sure there's no malware inside it. That takes a lot of computing power. Now consider the fact that virtually everything on the Internet is encrypted. Not just your bank account, but also Facebook, Google search, and YouTube.

A modern firewall has to have enough processing power and memory to push millions of packets through, open each one, and do "deep packet inspection" of encrypted data. These requirements go up every year. That's millions of calculations per second! You're not achieving that with a $49 device.

So, if you have a four- or five-year-old firewall, it probably doesn't have a chipset that *can* do this work. And it probably doesn't have a fast-enough processor or enough memory either. In other words, it has become the chokepoint on your network. And as more and more services are now cloud-based, you have more and more data that has to pass through this chokepoint.

Finally, I would like to encourage you to consider the "as a service" model. Imagine turning over all these headaches to us. For a flat fee, we'll make sure the firewall is up to spec. We'll make sure that processing power is centralized wherever it makes the most sense (in-house, in a co-location facility, or in the cloud). We'll make sure desktops are performing well and up to date. And so forth.

I can't help myself . . .

Sign right here and we'll take all these headaches off your hands . . .

33. Technicians must work in real time

What is "Real Time?" Quite simply, it means that technicians document everything as they go along. There are a couple of hard rules here, and an associated policy.

The first hard rule is that a technician will move a ticket to the *In Progress* status when they start working on a ticket. The associated policy is that each technician can only have one ticket In Progress at a time. So, for example, the service manager should never see more tickets In Progress than there are technicians at work today.

The second hard rule is that all notes and time entries must be entered into the ticket when the technician stops working on the ticket. Note: This is true whether the ticket is *Completed* or not! If a technician goes to lunch, sets a test to be run, or is waiting on a call from a vendor, they need to put notes in the ticket and move it to an appropriate status other than In Progress (e.g., "waiting on…").

There are two primary reasons for this requirement. One is important; the other is extremely important. The important reason is that the service board should always represent reality. For example, if a client calls and says, "I thought Karl was going to be here today to set up the conference room TV," the service manager (or office manager, for that matter) can look at the ticket and know whether Karl is on the way, working on the ticket now, or has already completed the job.

Note: It's a separate discussion of why Karl did not check in with the client upon leaving.

Where are each of your technicians right now, and what are they working on? That information should be immediately available in the ticketing system. This helps the service manager assign "next" tickets if necessary and be fully informed if clients call. If you choose to let the ticketing system track time automatically (not a best practice, in my opinion), then this policy will also keep those numbers as accurate as possible.

The extremely important reason for this policy is that it ensures that *notes* and *time entries* are up to date – up to the minute! Whether a ticket is closed or simply put in another status (e.g., waiting on parts, ready to work), the tech should put in notes about what was done up to that point. And the tech should enter the time worked on the ticket.

I am a big believer that you should track all the time in your business (see Chapter 30). This allows you to do wonderful things like determine tech utilization/billability, client profitability, etc. It also allows you to base your payroll on the time cards inside the PSA.

When employees track all of their time (8:00 AM to 5:00 PM) with no gaps and no overlaps, then you can determine exactly how much was spent on administrative work (e.g., meetings), service delivery, and personal time off. In this way, both external time (client facing) and internal time (for payroll) are visible in the PSA.

And the "real time" piece of this is most important because it's the only way to guarantee accuracy. There are only three ways to keep track of what you've done in a day. You might create a poster for this one:

Take perfect notes,
Have perfect recall,
or
Work in real time.

Technicians are not likely to take notes as they work, although I have seen it happen. Even if they do, it will be on some other device. It might be paper and pencil, cell phone notes, tablet, or laptop. But even then, these notes will need to be copied to the ticketing system. In my opinion, this adds an unnecessary step, takes additional time, and leaves room for error (such as forgetting to transfer notes).

No one has perfect recall. Seriously. Don't argue about this.

Luckily, technicians only have to do two things to make this procedure work perfectly. They need to move the ticket status to In Progress as soon as they start working on a ticket. And they need to put their notes and time into the ticket when they stop working on it.

That's it.

One trick we use to teach technicians to work in real time is to require a specific phrase at the end of each time entry. For us, the phrase was, "Documented work." Internally, to technicians and the service manager, that phrase means that a technician has verified the (updated) ticket status, entered time into the system, and entered relevant notes. Externally, clients simply see a note that the work was documented.

While there are advantages to the service manager in the middle of the day, the real benefit of this policy is that your system is always up to date and you never need to perform a big "fix-up" project that is tedious and completely non-billable.

If you or your techs think real-time notes and documentation take too much time, re-read Chapter 9: Slow down, get more done. It's better to keep up than to catch up.

34. Use a TSR Log

The Troubleshooting and Repair (TSR) Log is an extremely valuable tool for tracking issues, working with tech support from vendors, and documenting your work. We use a TSR Log whenever we build a server, when we call any vendor, and when a tech has worked on any issue for more than 30 minutes without making progress.

For newer technicians, we might require a TSR Log for any issue that causes more than 15 minutes work without progress. For senior techs, they should open an TSR Log and get help from somewhere after an hour.

In addition to being a GREAT documentation tool, the TSR Log is a great way to learn troubleshooting. It forces the user into thinking rigorously and documenting in such a way that you can effectively seek assistance from your co-workers or "tech support" on the other end of the phone.

By now I hope you've read Chapter Ten: *Know What You Know*. One of the important tools you have to help in this endeavor is the TSR Log.

With a TSR Log, you can state very clearly what you've tried and what the results were. You can make a change and then undo it with confidence because you have a map of where you've been. This is perfect for working with a manager, another technician, or a vendor. I have included sample TSR logs in *The Network Migration Workbook*, and in the *Managed Services Operations Manual*. It's also available to download within the Small Biz Thoughts Technology Community (www.smallbizthoughts.org).

Other than the cover sheet information (client, machine, issue, etc.), it is very straight forward. It's basically a series of lines with a date/time stamp on each line. This is so you can take elaborate notes and track the exact order of what you did.

Thus, as you're building a server or troubleshooting any problem, you have "perfect" notes (see the previous chapter). If anything goes wrong, you'll be able to document exactly what happened and where it happened in the process. This is very handy if you find yourself rebuilding that server from scratch someday. You're going to hit the same snag and it will be very handy to have quick access to the solution.

A TSR Log helps you keep very accurate information about how long it actually takes to build a server. This number will change over time as you gain experience and Microsoft releases updates. But even though this is a bit of a moving target, the more accurate your information, the more profitable you can make your next migration! (This is true because your time estimates will be more accurate.)

Creating a blank TSR Log sheet is easy. But it can be difficult to get everyone on your team to go along with the policy to use it. Over time, you need to support one another by asking "Did you have a TSR Log?" For us, this is important enough to impact quarterly reviews. If the service manager asks to see a TSR Log and there isn't one, that's a potential career-ending incident!

You should post a PDF version of your TSR Log on your company shared folder or drive, so technicians can access it easily from a client's office. We also require technicians to carry one printed out and ready to go at all times. We require them to use a TSR Log whenever they have been "stuck" on a problem for any amount of time.

To use the TSR Log, you need to simply fill out some key data and then proceed to take notes. There are two "triggers" for taking notes. One is whenever something significant happens. For example, when the server is rebooted, when a change is made, when an error occurs.

The second reason you enter something in the log is simply when you pass a fifteen-minute mark. Never let more than 15 minutes pass without an entry. It might simply be "Setup continued to unpack files." That way you know you didn't simply forget the log. But, more importantly, it will really help you pinpoint when things "go wrong" during an installation, configuration, troubleshooting, etc.

Once you have TSR Logs that have actually been used by technicians to solve problems, you'll need to deal with them properly. That means keeping all related notes together with the TSR Log. If you worked with a vendor to solve a problem, request a copy of their notes by email. This is true of Microsoft, Intel, HP, or anyone else you deal with.

Over time you'll see that your notes are MUCH better than theirs! Attach a copy of those notes to this document.

When the issue is resolved, three-hole punch this document and place it in the Tech Notes section of the Network Documentation Binder, or have an admin scan it into PDF format and store in the appropriate client folder.

In your PSA, annotate any related Service Tickets with a brief description of the problem and final resolution. Then simply refer to this TSR log by log number for full details on the issue.

For migration projects and server builds, you should probably keep a copy of the TSR Log in a file cabinet at your office. You can file by client/date, or simply keep all TSR logs together in one file drawer. Just make sure you can find it if you need it later.

If you're not used to TSR Logs, or rigorous note-taking, implementation of this policy might be difficult to execute. But stick with it and everyone on the team will get better at some of the most important things you do.

Remember: Most of your LOST labor comes from re-work and disorganized troubleshooting. TSR Logs can help you address both of those issues.

We all know that computers don't act randomly. They can't. So, when someone says that errors occur "randomly," they can't be correct. There's a pattern or a cause. We just can't see it.

With TSR Logs, we have a good chance of finding the pattern - and solving the problem - a lot faster!

35. Use a PSA (Professional Services Automation) Tool

You need a ticketing system. But you need more than that: a PSA.

In any industry, we see LOBs – Line of Business applications, such as Dentrix, Yardi, or IMIS. One way or another, these tools are a form of CRM (customer relationship management) tool. In the IT world, we tend to call our systems PSAs.

This is the one tool most specifically designed to help you build a technology consulting business. On top of managing tickets, a PSA will help you manage client information, employee information, and service delivery generally.

A PSA is a program (or service) for keeping track of all information related to your consulting service. This includes most or all of the following:

- Clients
  - Client Contacts
  - Client Technology Configurations
- Contracts
- Billing
- Employees
  - Employee Time / Payroll
  - Internal Tasks
- Service Requests / Service Tickets / Cases
- Projects
- Reporting
- Accounting
- Customer Relationship Management / Sales
- . . . and more.

The Service Board is a subset of the PSA. When you look through my 4-volume set of books on SOPs (*The Managed Services Operations Manual*), you'll find excruciating detail about all the things you should be doing inside your PSA. As you can guess from the list above, this includes:

- Tracking your employees
  - . . . and all their activities
  - . . . and their billable time (and non-billable time)
- Tracking your clients
  - . . . and all your interactions with them
  - . . . and all their technology/computer systems
- Tracking all the work you need to do
  - . . . internally and externally
- Tracking all your contracts
- Tracking all your sales
- Connecting to all the other tools and services you use to run your business
- Reporting all of the above
- . . . and more.

Choosing Your PSA

No matter how large or small your consulting business is, you should have a system for tracking all this stuff. A PSA designed for your business is a great investment.

Today there are literally dozens of systems you can use to run your business. The "800 Pound Gorillas" are Autotask (Datto) and ConnectWise.

Some other contenders include TigerPaw, SolarWinds, Atera, Ninja, and Halo. And, of course, you can use a wide variety of CRM products that are not necessarily intended for the IT industry.

I encourage you to look at several options and determine which is best for your company. You should also talk to other IT professionals and see what they are using.

Among the dozens of tools available for running your business, you will find that they each have a different subset of features. You need to make sure that the one you pick is not missing significant features. They might be excellent at managing the help desk, for example, but don't integrate with QuickBooks, Xero, or Sage. Or they are primarily a CRM tool and don't integrate contract management or employee time tracking.

When you talk to successful IT service providers, you'll see that they almost universally use the PSA for almost every aspect of running their business.

And by the way, don't worry about making a mistake. Your business will be much better off as soon as you invest in any PSA and begin using it to run your business! You can change brands. I have, more than once.

Use Your PSA's Knowledgebase

This advice is almost to the level of being an unbreakable rule. Generally speaking, you need to have some kind of master knowledgebase where your employees can find all the information they need about clients, documentation, procedures, etc.

You can buy a separate product for this (e.g., IT Glue, Liongard, or PassPortal). Or you can use a more generic platform such as SharePoint or even the files and folders within your cloud storage. But if you use a PSA, remember that it already has a documentation system built in.

There are two competing "truths" when it comes to databases like this. First, you should only track things that you will actually run a report on. Don't waste your time putting useless information in the system. Second, if you ever decide to run a report, you need to already have the information in the system. As Homer Simpson would say: "Doh!"

Luckily, there are some core things you just have to put in the system, or let the RMM put in for you. This includes basic client contact information as well as all the device configurations. You don't need to over-document, but it's very handy to know if you're looking at an HP desktop or an Apple laptop.

If you keep excellent notes inside your ticketing system, then you'll have lots of good documentation there. But most PSAs aren't very good at digging through old tickets to find something. But they are good at digging through the built-in knowledgebase that ships with the PSA.

You need to decide which information you wish to enter and keep. You need to document this list as a standard operating procedure, and you need to train your technicians to track these things.
Make your PSA as usable as possible!

Section VIII
Rules for Service Tickets

36. Track ALL Time Inside Your Business

37. All Work Is Done on a Service Ticket

38. Every Ticket Is Massaged Every Time It's Touched

39. Every Job Has a Scope

40. Document Absolutely Everything

36. Track ALL Time Inside Your Business

To me, this advice is so critical to a service business that I have built hour-long training sessions around it. In fact, when I teach about KPIs (key performance indicators), they are more about time than about money. But that's because of this truth: How you spend your time is the most visible indicator of how you spend your money.

"Time is your widget." – Manuel Palachuk

My brother Manuel worked with me in one of my businesses for six years. We are, as a result, very close together in our approach to managing a service business. When he says time is your widget, he means it is the raw material you use to make your product.

If you were making shoes, you would buy leather, put your skills into it, and out would come shoes. If you're making pizza, you would buy flour and olive oil, make dough, and out would come pizza. In a service business, you buy labor from your employees and you sell labor to your clients, even if it's for a flat fee.

What's the thing in the middle that you've added your magic to so that an $18-an-hour technician (what you buy) becomes a $150-an-hour technician (what you sell)? The magic that you've added to it in the middle, the part that you have created, is **the entire collection of all your values, processes, and procedures**. It is your brand.

As we discussed in Section II, your brand is not your logo. Your brand is every single thing you do in your company—the way you talk to clients, the way that you communicate with clients, the way you present yourself, the way your technicians dress, the way that you work a service agreement. It's every single thing you do.

The value you add to your employees' labor is your brand. The value of your brand creates something that is more valuable than what the employees could do by themselves.

For most service businesses, labor is the most expensive thing you buy (from your employees). And it's probably the most profitable thing you sell. As a result, tracking time is extremely important.

And let me be honest right now, so you don't have to feel bad: You will only take this seriously if you believe it. If you just flat out disagree, then you won't track your time and you won't enforce having your employees track their time.

Time tracking literally has to come from the top down. You have to believe that it's important and that you can use it to measure every meaningful piece of your profitability. The owner has to believe. The managers have to believe. And the employees have to believe.

If you don't believe, you won't do it.

It's also important that no one on your team sees this as a "control" issue. If you have a vision in your head of you standing at the door giving the evil-eye to every employee as they file in, one at a time, and punch a time card, then you're on the wrong track.

We don't track time to control people or because we don't trust them. It actually has nothing to do with either of those things. (Remember Chapter 23: You can't control people, but you can control your processes.)

We track time in order to make sure we're using it properly, and to determine how profitable we are. Remember the client we fired in Chapter 28, the one that was worth $150,000 in revenue but only $27,000 in profit? We made that calculation in short order because we tracked time extremely well.

If you've got a $10,000 project, but spend $9,000 in labor, you have a very low-profit project! But if you have a $10,000 project and spend only $2,000 in labor, you have a very high-profit project.

How do you know which one you have?

You track all the time inside your business.

Way at the beginning of the book, I mentioned Simon Sinek's book, *Start with Why*. Here's an example of where you can apply that. Technicians need to know why you track time. And they need to know it's about effective service delivery and profit—not being a control freak.

This is so important that you might have an administrative assistant whose job includes examining time cards to verify there are no gaps and no overlaps for job times. That admin also needs to know *why* you do that. It's about performance, metrics, billability, and profitability.

Other rules follow from this (see the next few chapters). All work has to be done within a service ticket. All the tickets have to be accurate, all the time. All the tickets also have to have a well-defined scope of work. And all that work needs to be documented.

The big picture of how you manage time is also the big picture of how your company makes money (or not).

Every service ticket must have an accurate time estimate.

I assume you have some way to track work. If not, solve that problem before you do anything else, because I 100% guarantee you are losing money. I'm going to assume that your process for tracking work involves some kind of ticketing system. And so, each thing that needs to get done will be in a separate ticket.

So, let's say you have a ticketing system. Each thing you need to do internally or for a client is in a ticket. Those tickets need to have accurate time estimates. What does that mean?

Let's say you have a job ticket. Fill in the specifics for your industry. The job ticket will include figuring out the specifics of the service request, acquiring parts or other resources, fixing the problem (or doing the maintenance), and documenting what you did.

Some tickets will take fifteen minutes. Some will take an hour. Some will take ten hours. Some will take an hour for analysis and another three hours after you get the parts. Whatever the case, you need to do your best to put an accurate time estimate into every ticket. Here's why.

Eventually, you will run a report of all of the time that's in your system. This is your backlog report. Some people don't like the term "backlog" because they think it suggests that the goal is to be zero. Your backlog should never be zero! If it's zero, you're out of business. Here are the pieces of your backlog report. Whatever system you use for tracking tickets or tasks may be different, but this information should be in there somewhere:

(Note: Time means time remaining on the ticket.)

Ticket #	Client	Job Description	Time
1234	ABC Corp.	Job . . .	1:00
1235	BCD Inc.	Job . . .	4:00
1236	CDE Corp.	Job . . .	12:00
1237	DEF Inc.	Job . . .	4:00
1238	ABC Corp.	Job . . .	17:30
1239	CDE Corp.	Job . . .	9:00
. . . (etc.)			
		Total Time:	100:00

Backlog is simply all of the labor inside your system. It's the work that needs to be done.

Backlog should never be zero, but backlog should be manageable. What does that mean?

Let's say you are the owner or the manager of the service department. If you're lucky, you can "deliver" four hours of legit work on a service ticket per week. You have to deal with customer service, managing employees, payroll, sales, and all kinds of other stuff.

Now let's look at your service department.

Your best technician is 80% "billable." That means she provides about thirty-two hours of work on tickets per week. Awesome.

Your second technician is 60% billable. He's decent but not awesome. That's okay. He still provides about twenty-four hours of work on tickets per week.

Finally, your third technician is a newbie. He's 50% billable and learning the ropes. He can deliver about twenty hours of work on tickets per week.

Total (you and three techs): Your team can knock out about eighty hours per week.

You will work through most of your hundred-hour backlog this week, and should finish it early next week.

Sidebar: Where did the other time go?

Why isn't everyone billing forty hours per week? Aren't you paying them? And more importantly, why aren't you irritated about it?

Simple answer: This is the real world. No one is one hundred percent billable.

You hold meetings that cannot be charged to a client. You might pay people to do internal tasks (like clean up the work bench).

Sometimes, technicians go out on jobs that are not billable. You might not charge clients for travel time. You might pay people to sit in training sessions.

In other words, there's a certain overhead to running a business. There just is. On top of that, some people are good, some are better, and some are best. You can work to improve people, but that's probably training time you are paying for that you don't bill to a client.

(End of Sidebar)

Time also flows IN.

So, your team is able to knock out about eighty hours per week from the backlog. But, of course, new tickets are open every day.

How fast does time flow *into* your business? There's only one way to know: You need to track it.

Every day, someone needs something. Does time come in at a nice and easy eighty hours per week? That would be nice, right? You could pretty much guarantee that every job would be done in seven or eight work days. But, again, we live in the real world.

Some weeks, you get a nice eighty hours of new time in your backlog. But some weeks it drops to sixty hours. And some weeks it shoots up to more than a hundred hours. When you sell big projects, it jumps way up.

If you watch your backlog report, it will be like watching someone breathe. Time flows in. Time flows out. In and out. It's your business breathing in and breathing out.

Once you know the average rate of how your backlog breathes in and out each week, you can figure out lots of other things. What will happen when one of your technicians takes a week off? Obviously, it depends on how many "billable" hours they produce per week.

And when you sell a big project, when can it be delivered? When can you start and when will it be done?

Oh, and when do you need to hire someone? When do you have more backlog than is acceptable and normal for your business?

Similarly, when is it time to cut back on someone's hours because the work just isn't coming in?

And we've skipped over a big question: What *should* your backlog be? Of course, I can't answer that for you. You need to examine your business, and your service board, and determine what "normal" looks like.

You do all of these things by measuring the time inside your ticketing system and the time worked by your employees. In other words, by tracking all the time in your business!

Project Estimates

There's one other really important thing you can do with accurate time measurements: Create accurate project estimates!

Let's look at your team. For this example, we'll drop you because you don't really provide much sellable labor. And we'll add in another tech who is 70% billable. Here's your new team:

Tech One	80%	(32 hours/week)
Tech Two	70%	(28 hours/week)
Tech Three	60%	(24 hours/week)
Tech Four	50%	(20 hours/week)

Please understand what this means from two different perspectives. First, you are paying for 160 hours of labor per week. These folks can deliver about 104 hours of labor on tickets per week. So, the team as a whole is 65% billable. Got it?

Second, that means you need to buy about 1.5 hours of labor for every hour you sell to a client or use on a project. Do the math.

If a project is 20 hours, you'll need to buy 20/.65 = 31 hours.
If a project is 50 hours, you'll need to buy 50/.65 = 77 hours.
If a project is 104 hours, you'll need to buy 100/.65 = 160 hours.

So now you can create even more accurate cost estimates for projects. This allows you to do better planning and virtually guarantee that you won't have unprofitable projects. At least not because of bad cost estimating.

Now look at all the other calculations you can do. Once you track all the time in your business, you can determine:

- The profitability of each technician
- The profitability of each contract
- The profitability of each project
- The profitability of each client
- The profitability of each ticket

Beware "Missing" Time

One final warning: all means all. You can't track some or most of your time and get a usable numbers. In my experience, *most* service businesses make this mistake.

Until you track 100% of your time, you don't know how much of your time you are tracking. By definition, percentages are based on 1.0 = 100%.

This is not about getting your algebra wrong. The formula matters because this is how it proceeds:

- All technicians (employees who deliver labor)
- Must track 100% of their time
- During their shift
- There must be no gaps
- Or overlaps

If you do this, you will be able to use your ticketing system as your payroll tracking system.

A few notes about types of time. First, and most importantly, there's "billable" time. This really means productive labor in service of the client. You might send an invoice or include it in a flat-fee project or contract. The important thing is that it's not one of the other types of time.

Second, there's admin time. This includes meetings, sales calls, training, clean-up, etc. You pay your employees for a lot of little stuff that cannot be billed to a client or contract. Note that required breaks are admin time because you're still paying the employee.

Third, there's personal time. This is not labor you buy. So, for example, meal time is not paid for most companies. So while it's outside the time an employee is paid, we still need to track it?

Why? Because you need to make sure this time was not spent on a client contract! Let's say that someone takes off an hour early to see their kid's play. No problem. Just make sure it goes in the system as personal time. You're not paying the employee, but you also know that you're not invoicing a client.

If you only track billable time (the greatest temptation), you have no way of knowing whether the missing hours were admin time, personal time, or time with a client that you are not invoicing.

37. All Work Is Done on a Service Ticket

I used to tell my technicians, "A service ticket is just a bucket into which clients can place money. If there is no bucket, there's no place for them to pay us."

Fundamentally, a ticketing system allows us to have perfect visibility about what we are doing to deliver service to our clients. At least that's the ideal. So, let's say, we can have perfect visibility if we set up the ticketing system the right way, use it fully and consistently, and generate the reports we need.

What do I mean by "visibility?" There are several pieces to this. First, if every single thing that needs to be done is entered into the ticketing system, then we can see and understand how much work we have (that is, backlog). This visibility makes it possible for the service manager to make good decisions and guide the process.

Second, when technicians work tickets, they enter their time and their notes into the system. This has three great benefits. It allows us to see exactly what was done to fix the problem; it helps us justify our billing to the client; and it allows us to track how time is used by our staff.

Third, and more broadly, putting all that information *into* the system makes it possible for us to generate reports and get information *out* of the system.

When I say all work must be done on a ticket, I simply mean that the ticket must be created first. You cannot ever pick up the phone and start giving support to a client. First, you need to take sixty seconds and create a ticket. That interrupt-driven mindset always costs you money.

Creating a ticket first is fast and easy. Let's say you pick up the phone and a client needs help. You simply train your technicians to say the words, "Have you already created a ticket, or do you want me to create a ticket?"

Some people argue that this is unnecessary for simple little tasks. Therefore, they argue, you don't need a ticket for a three-minute task. This is an example of trying to figure out guidelines based on the exception instead of the rule.

Let's be honest: Most jobs are not three minutes. But even if they were, you still need to record how you spend your time. Was it billable or covered by a service contract? Someone has to pay for that time! Will it be you or the client?

Remember: When time is not billable to a client or contract, it will be paid for by you, the owner. Period.

In addition to that, you need a record of what was actually done. Did the client receive useful information or labor? Great. You need to document that. Remember, you are always nurturing an on-going relationship with the client.

So, if they call again in three months and say "that thing" is happening again, and they want to know how to fix it, you need to be able to look in your ticketing system and give them the answer. If you say, "I have no record that you called us about that, or that we helped you out," you will look incompetent.

Remember: You always want to build processes and procedures that are scalable. Not creating tickets, not tracking time, and not keeping track of what you did are all very bad habits if you want to create a scalable system.

Take, for example, every large corporation you work with. When you call for support, they ask you some basic information (name, account number, address, etc.). They are creating a ticket so that they can track the problem, the progress, and the resolution. Again, this takes less than sixty seconds. And now work can begin.

One Task per Ticket

Also remember: Tickets need to be properly constructed. That means that you have one task per ticket. Each ticket should have a title and a short description. Depending on the system you're using, you might also have a long description.

A good title and short description will give an excellent idea of the problem. A bad title or description will say something like "Bob Johnson" or "123 Elm Street—plumbing."

Several local service companies now handle heating, air conditioning, plumbing, and electrical. I sincerely hope they don't use the same technicians for all of that. But whatever they do, their tickets need to give some kind of clue about what the actual problem is.

In the world of IT, for example, "Lisa's computer" is a bad title for a ticket. "Outlook opens in safe mode" is a good title. It gives some idea of what you can expect.

The golden rule for any ticketing system is: One task per ticket! Sometimes you have larger maintenance jobs (e.g., monthly maintenance or quarterly maintenance) that combine a lot of various tasks. But most of the time, you want to keep each task separate. The reason is simple: You never know which task will spin out of control and become a major problem unto itself.

When all work is done on a service ticket, you know what your company needs to do, what you have done, how long it took, and how much labor you had to buy to get it all done. On top of all that, you have all the notes and details, so you can reconstruct the problem and the solution.

As my friend Richard Tubb likes to say,

"The mind is a terrible place to store information."

(https://richardtubb.co.uk/)

38. Every Ticket Is Massaged Every Time It's Touched

Let's take a step back and look at service tickets very broadly. No matter what industry you're in, a service ticket will include this basic information (some of which is optional):

- Date ticket opened
- Customer name
- Customer contact information
- (Company name)
- Problem (ticket title)
- Short description
- (Long description)
- Additional notes
- Time estimate*
- Status**

*The time estimate is your best educated guess about how much labor will be required.

**The status will define where the ticket is along the path to completion. Statuses will probably include In progress, Waiting on Parts, Scheduled, Assigned, Completed, Closed, and others specific to your company.

In addition, depending on the specifics of your industry and the software you're using, a ticket may include:

- Priority—High, Medium, Low
- Work type/sub-type
- Service level (if escalation is part of your process)
- Work queue or service board
- Related sales

- Related tickets or projects
- Customer contract
- Bill rate

Massaging Your Tickets

By "massage" we simply mean that we're going to look at each ticket in the system and make sure it has the correct information—priority, status, contract, bill rate, time estimate, and so forth. When you check through these items, each ticket becomes more accurate every time somebody looks at it.

In my experience, the single biggest problem with any ticketing system is the **status**. When I coach companies on their service board, the engagement always (100% of the time) starts by eliminating many tickets that should be "closed" or "completed" but are in some other status. Note that every other status means that the tickets look like they're still in need of work instead of being completed.

Aside from status, the most important details to keep up to date are *priority* and *time estimate*. If priorities are meaningful, then you need to make sure that high priority jobs are getting high priority attention. And if your time estimates are up to date, then you can run accurate reports about your backlog, which will help with scheduling employees, projects, etc.

Invariably, if no one is in charge of keeping the service board in good condition, it will deteriorate to the point where it is almost useless. This is not an exaggeration. When I work to clean up a service board, I usually find lots of old tickets that should just be closed or deleted.

Most of the time, this is caused by the bad habits of the owner or the service manager—whichever has ultimate control of the service board. "Micro-managing" owners and lazy service managers allow tickets to just grow old without closing them. This is often because someone is waiting for "the boss" to approve the charges or adjust something.

I can't tell you how often I find tickets for clients who haven't been clients for six months or more! And, of course, that means that the time estimates are complete fiction, as is the average ticket age and the average time to complete a ticket.

The promise of a service board is that you will be more profitable. You will be able to see exactly what needs to be done, which clients are the most profitable, which work pays the best, which technicians are the most efficient, and so forth. But if your ticketing system is a jumbled mess, then you can't tell any of these things.

I recommend three "rules" to keep tickets up to spec:

1) Every ticket is massaged every time it's touched.
2) Someone should do a light-touch massage every day.
3) The service manager should do a deep-issue massage once per week.

Rule one means that everyone—including administrative assistants, sales people, and service techs—should be conscientious about keeping tickets updated. As long as you're going to open a ticket and look at it, give it a quick glance and make sure it looks right. This is a five-second chore and should just be part of what everyone does.

Rule two is an actual assigned task. Someone should get an overview of the tickets each day. How many are new? How many were closed yesterday? If you have a process to "complete" tickets and then move them to invoice review before closing, someone needs to make sure that happens.

Rule three is the weekly deep-issue massage. This should be performed by the service manager, who should have a thorough understanding of the state of the service board. Basically, this job consists of sorting and re-sorting the service tickets, looking for problems and making sure everything is up to date.

For example, you will sort all tickets by priority and see if you have too many high-priority tickets, and also make sure that the low-priority jobs are actually getting some attention. Then, sort it by age to make sure you don't have a bunch of really old tickets. Sort by client to make sure that you don't have one client that's got an unreasonable number of tickets. If you do, plan to send somebody out there for a day.

Sort your tickets every way that you can from every direction. You will literally get a 360-degree view of what your board looks like. Again, the service manager is the one person in your company that should absolutely master the knowledge about what's going on with your service board.

Depending on how many tickets you have, and how much of a mess you have, the first deep-issue massage might take an hour a day for a week. But once you have it cleaned up, the weekly job will be just a few minutes. Maybe fifteen minutes, maximum.

Note: This skill is another that's infinitely scalable. When you get to the point when you've got a thousand tickets in the system, the skill doesn't change. The sorting doesn't change, although it takes a little bit longer.

You'll find that it's pretty easy to clean up the board, and to keep it cleaned up. Once you get to the point where your service board truly represents the work that needs to be done, it suddenly becomes a very useful tool.

The issues that got you off-track are easy to keep at bay. Tickets will get closed. Priorities will be accurate. Time estimates become a meaningful measure of backlog. The work you do—and the work to-be-done—become visible inside your ticketing system.

This cultural change is easy to implement and easy to keep up. Just do it.

39. Every Job Has a Scope

No matter what business you're in, you know that "projects" can get out of control. Projects can be estimated incorrectly and managed poorly. The worst problems with projects are that they are over time (delivered late), over budget, or that they simply never end. Contractors often disappear for no reason and then re-appear and have to re-work part of the project.

The single worst problem with projects is *scope creep*. That's when a little project gets morphed into a different, and often larger project. And since this is a book for service providers and not their customers, let me be very honest: The customer is almost always fifty percent responsible for this scope creep.

Often, customers have unreasonable expectations and small budgets (or no budget at all). They don't want to pay for the design part of the project. So work starts without a map. Of course it's going to go in the wrong direction!

All of this—ALL of this—can be avoided with good communication and mutually agreed-upon scope of work that is enforced with additional good communication.

(Note: My friend Dana Goulston and I wrote a book on project management that lays out a process for staying inside the scope and virtually guaranteeing success. See *Project Management in Small Business*.)

Well, the same is true with simple service tickets. They can be poorly managed and therefore very unprofitable. In most cases, these problems are due to scope creep, communications, and managing expectations.

Here's a perfect example from early in my consulting career. I went to a client's office to set up a simple workstation, which I estimated at one hour of labor. He had brought in a separate machine from home that he had tried to install a hard drive into. He asked if I could look at it.

Well, I did the workstation first. Once it was successful, I opened up the home computer. This was back in the days when installing a hard drive involved making changes to switches and jumpers on both the motherboard and the drives. He had messed with everything and it took quite a while to get it straightened out.

Once I was successful, I handed him an invoice for three hours work—and he was furious! I remember his exact complaint: It took me three hours to set up a simple desktop computer! I must be completely incompetent.

I found myself justifying my actions and spelling out exactly what happened—without pointing out that he was an incompetent computer repairman. But even in the moment, I knew this was 100% my fault.

I should have finished the first job and presented an invoice, then started the second job and a second invoice. Remember this extremely important piece of wisdom: You never know when a job is going to go very, very bad. It may be your fault or not your fault. But "stuff happens"—and sometimes it happens to you. Remember this!

Two Tattoos

When I teach project management, I always tell people, "You should get two tattoos. On your right arm you should get a tattoo that says 'inside the scope' and on your left arm one that says 'outside the scope.' If you could remember those two things you can stay profitable in every project."

I will give the gold nugget from our project management book: Projects that stay inside the scope stay profitable; projects outside the scope may or may not be profitable. But, barring bad project management, all unprofitable projects are outside the scope.

Here's what happens: You're working a project and somebody says, "Oh, as long as you're here, and everybody's in the office today, let's go ahead and . . . [throw new work on your plate]."

No, let's not.

Remember: Your clients don't really understand your job. They have some idea of what you do, but they have no idea about what is related to what; they don't know how complicated things are, or how long they take; and it all looks simple from the outside because you're good at what you do.

Clients are not ill-intentioned when they ask you to do additional work. They don't know what they don't know!

There are basically three things that can happen with "new" requests that come up in the middle of a job:

1) What you are doing now (inside the original service ticket) fixes the additional problem the client has.
2) The new request is extremely small and easy and you take one or two minutes and just do it as part of the current ticket.
3) You simply note that the request is outside the scope of the current ticket and you create a separate service ticket.

Why? Why not just change the ticket and do the additional work? The primary reason is:

You never know when a job is going to go very, very bad. It may be your fault or not your fault. But "stuff happens"—and sometimes it happens to you. (I told you to remember this.)

The whole concept of scope creep is a common and recurring plot for situation comedies. You've seen it. The hero calls in a handyman who proceeds to break the plumbing, the floors, the roof, and everything else. What started as a simple job becomes a nightmare—and sometimes a feature film starring Tom Hanks and Shelley Long.

There are two simple rules that will keep your tickets as profitable as possible. First, you must define the ticket scope properly. That means it is clear and precise. It has limits and it will be obvious when you are successful.

Second, no one is allowed to change the scope. In other words, no scope creep. That means no one—not you, not your technicians, and not the client. No one can change the scope. *But* anyone can create a new service ticket!

Remember the worst complaints clients have. When you stay inside the scope, each specific job can be delivered on time, inside the budget you promised. And, most importantly, the job can come to a successful conclusion.

This entire section has been about Service Tickets. And, in the end, everything relies on having a clearly defined scope for each ticket. That allows you to have an accurate title, job description, and time estimate. Those allow you to manage how time flows inside your service board.

As I mentioned earlier, you can't have a ticket that says "Larry's computer." The ticket has to be specific, it's got to have a good title, and it's got to make sense, and you can't throw everything into the bundle.

Now, get thee to a tattoo parlor.

40. Document Absolutely Everything

What is "documentation?" In a service business, it means many things. It means writing out your processes and procedures. It means keeping track of all the work that needs to be done (in service tickets). It means reporting what was actually done in response to each ticket. It means keeping track of client equipment and configurations. It means tracking time.

In short, it means everything.

Remember that one of your goals is to create a business that is scalable. Even if you don't want to "grow" much, being scalable means that you are able to take on more clients. And if you do want to grow, it means that you can replicate your successful habits with new clients, new employees, and even new locations.

Remember Section II, above: Branding is everything you do. Documenting what you do and how you do it defines and protects your brand. "Your way" of doing things is what separates you from the competition.

If you were to buy a franchise, part of what you buy is corporate branding and marketing. But most of what you buy is documentation. What color are the carpets and counters? How do you count out the till at the end of the night? How do you greet customers? And so forth.

How do you do absolutely everything in your business? You document everything, and you build your business and culture around that documentation.

I know many readers are saying "ugh" right now. You didn't get into business to spend all your time writing stuff down. Fine. But this is the reality of the world.

If you have to remember everything, then there is a hard limit on your ability to grow. The very existence of documentation allows you to grow your business.

In my first IT consulting business, I had been in business about five years before I had my first full-time employee. He was very technical, but he was impressed that I had memorized so much client information. But I would not let him rely on me for this information: It was written down.

I had about twenty clients under contract at the time, and I'd memorized all the server names, which Internet service provider each of them used, their IP addresses, their DNS information, and most usernames and all the passwords we had access to.

But if my technician asked for a server, IP address, or anything else, I only had one answer: It's in the network documentation workbook. There are two primary reasons for this answer. First, I wanted him to rely on that documentation, and to value it tremendously. Second, I knew that my business would never grow beyond the smallest chokepoint. And my memory is a pretty small chokepoint.

Over time, we developed a system of documentation that could be expanded far beyond twenty, two hundred, or even two thousand clients. As long as you are consistent, there should be no limit to your ability to document client operations.

The same goes for our internal processes.

Let's look at the big picture for a minute so this discussion of documentation makes sense in the context of your business. At some point, you start with the vision for your company and why it exists. Then you have overall policies. Policies are the high-level guiding principles for your business.

With luck, you'll look at the contents of this book and adopt many of these "rules" as your policies. For example, "We get prepaid for everything we do," or "Do not be interrupt-driven."

Policies like that make up the big picture. Next, you need to look at specific processes and procedures. Processes, procedures, and checklists are the tools you use to turn policies into visible activities and service delivery within your company.

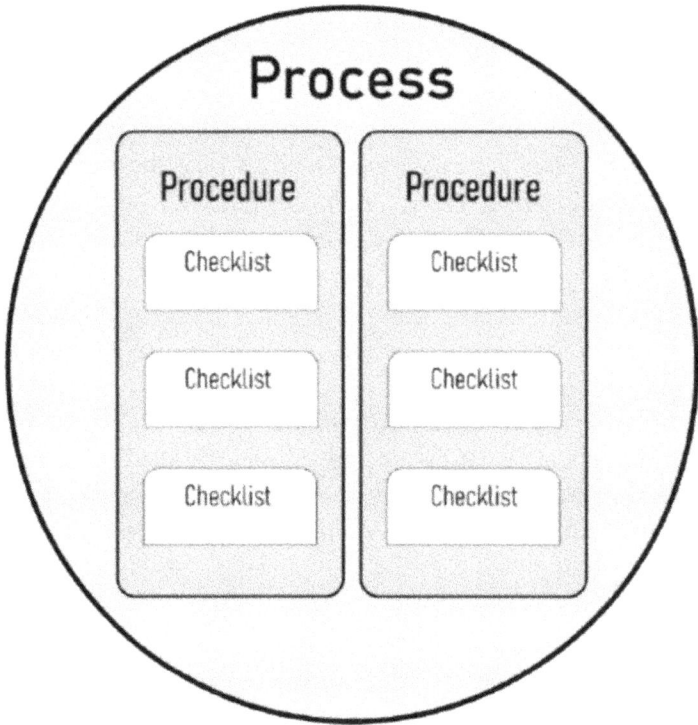

Process

Procedure	Procedure
Checklist	Checklist
Checklist	Checklist
Checklist	Checklist

A few definitions are in order.

A Policy states your intentions and your philosophy about a topic.

A Process is the name given to a series of tasks that result in a general outcome.

A Procedure is the name given to a specific set of action steps that achieve a specific outcome. A process might include several different procedures.

A Checklist is the name given to the finest level of detail for executing the action steps needed to achieve a result. A procedure should include at least one checklist.

As you can see from the illustration, these elements are nested. Processes contain procedures and procedures contain checklists. Let's look at an example.

Example: Employee Hiring Process

In the big picture, there is a hiring process. It probably includes a procedure to find candidates, a procedure for weaning the list of candidates, a procedure for interviewing, a procedure for evaluating, a procedure for negotiating an offer, and a procedure for onboarding the employee.

Each of these procedures will have one or more checklists. For example, once you begin to bring someone onboard, you will need a checklist to prepare for their arrival (print out paperwork, determine whether they need keys or security codes, assign a parking spot, etc.). You will also need a checklist to make sure all of the "day one" tasks have been completed (filled out that paperwork, introduced to the staff, toured the office, assigned a desk, etc.).

The hiring process is a great example of a "process" that most people don't do well until they've hired several people. All too often, in small business, we hire someone and then have done zero preparation for their first day.

So, the new employee sits and watches the boss work until the boss has time to actually give them something to do. And even then, it's just "something" and not necessarily something important.

It is a far better experience for the employee if you have all of their first day tasks laid out before they show up. The paperwork is ready, their desk is ready, and so forth.

As always, *you do already have a process for all this*. It just might not be consistent. It might not be written down. There might not be a checklist. And, therefore, you might execute it a little differently each time.

Processes do not exist simply to create bureaucracy. A process is a collection of activities that accomplishes a goal. Be clear on your goals, and be consistent in the processes that advance those goals.

. . . And one final point:

Remember that your processes are designed to *build your brand*. If you don't have processes in place, your employees will do their best to give good service—but they will each be doing things their own way. They will be building *their* brand, not your brand.

It really is as simple as this: Everyone reading this book can make a sandwich. But unless you've got Subway's bread, Subway's ingredients, and Subway's training, you can't make a Subway sandwich.

Build your brand: Document everything you do.

Section IX
The Bigger, Bigger Picture

41. Relax Focus Succeed™

42. Why Does Your Business Exist?

43. The Culture of Success

41. Relax Focus Succeed™

One of my books (my favorite, in fact) is called *Relax Focus Succeed*. It spells out my philosophy about work-life balance. I believe that it is essential to balance your personal life and your work life.

On one hand, I believe you *have to do this* in order to be truly successful. Every single time you talk to someone who hates their job and is completely stressed out about work, I guarantee that they've lost this balance—or never had it. And this is particularly bad when they're the boss or owner, and they create the job they hate!

On the other hand, I also know from experience that you can create a job and a life that are in balance because they have been designed to be that way. I'm not saying that's easy to create, or particularly easy to maintain. But it is absolutely possible.

I wrote down in January of 2011: I want to write more, I want to speak more, I want to travel more. And I gradually re-designed my business and my life, so that's what I do.

I make a living writing books (and blog posts and white papers, and lots of activities that flow from there). I speak twenty to thirty times per year in front of audiences all over the world. Of course, that involves travel. Unless there's a global pandemic, I visit more than twenty cities in three or four different countries every year.

In my industry there are a lot of "road warriors" who travel more than I. But almost none of them have built *balance* into their lifestyle. They fly across the country—or across the globe—and then immediately fly somewhere else. They don't actually visit the city they're in, and rarely see anything except the conference hotel.

I can't do that. I mean I actually, physically cannot do that. I have rheumatoid arthritis, an immune disease that causes the body to attack itself. It makes me tired much of the time and limits how much physical activity I can do.

When I travel, I always add a day or two in each city. This allows me to regroup, recoup, and do a good job once I hit the stage. It also allows me to actually see the places I visit. It is a great balance.

I wrote *Relax Focus Succeed* after I went through a very strange period in my life. I was diagnosed with RA at age thirty-nine. At that time, I was working very hard, growing my consulting business.

On top of that, we were moving from one house to another and I was working every evening to get the new house ready to move in. After the move, I spent the evenings converting the old house into a rental unit.

As the disease took hold, I was more tired and more sore every day. And the medicines I took were truly debilitating. With RA, the immune system goes into overdrive, attacking the joints and causing great pain and swelling.

The drugs used to fight RA are designed to beat down the immune system. And they have side effects that are almost as bad as the disease. It took a few years for me to get the right mix of drugs and physical activity to be able to work five or six hours per day.

Somewhere in those years, I grew my company, started two other businesses, wrote three books, and became successful by most peoples' standards. More importantly, I was personally happy and fulfilled.

This transition is not a coincidence. Quite the contrary. It is from the depths of my illness that I discovered the formula for personal and professional success. *Relax Focus Succeed* was written to help others find this balance—without the chronic disease! I don't mean a path to money, but a path of true success: to happiness, fulfillment, and balance.

Why This Matters

Let me be very honest about my motivations here. I consider myself a spiritual person. I believe we need to serve ourselves and serve others in this world.

I also came to grips with my mortality sooner than most people. My father died when I was twenty-three and he was fifty. He had his first heart attack at forty. And while I did not have a sense of impending doom, I realized that we are on this earth for a very short time—and we need to get to work on whatever it is we wish to achieve.

Over the years, I have known a number of people who died far too young. My good friend Scott is a perfect example. He was married for the first time at age thirty-seven. And he died in a scuba incident four months later. He actually achieved a good deal in his life. But you can't escape the fact that that was a short amount of time to serve yourself or others.

I have been lucky to be successful in almost everything I've done. I've managed companies and departments for large organizations. I've built several businesses. My grown daughter is very successful and well-rounded.

But, luck aside, none of this happened by accident. My motto is:

Nothing Happens by Itself

You need to set your intentions and then let those intentions guide your goals and activities. You need to have a "big picture" for your life. With a big picture, you might be able to reach your goals. Without a big picture, there really are no goals to achieve.

Your life should be much more than existing every day so you can get up and exist the next day, and the next.

Existence is fine. Don't get me wrong. I'm a big fan. But it's not enough. You should exist for a reason. And you can pray and meditate and get advice from others, but in the end, you need to determine the reason for your life.

Your goals do not need to be grand. You don't have to save the world or eliminate poverty. But there should be *some* goals. You should have *some* reason for doing what you do.

Some people will tell you that all this "work-life balance" stuff is a bunch of nonsense. They say you need to work as hard as you can, even if it means destroying your family, because you only have the energy of youth for a short time. So, push as hard as you can. You can spend time on a personal life later.

This is silly (as you may recall, that's the nice word I use so I'm not accused of calling people stupid).

First, there are about five billion examples of people who ignored and destroyed their families because they focused so much on work that their families faded away or simply got on with their lives and left the workaholic shouting, "You ingrates! I've done all of this for you."

Second, workaholism kills. There's massive amounts of research behind this. Workaholism increases incidents of heart disease, stress, cancer, and just about any ailment they have ever researched. It destroys people. It destroys families. And it's not really good for business!

Remember, two of the recurring themes we've seen in this book: Successful businesses need to be *scalable* and *sustainable*. Both of those goals will lead you to create a business that doesn't kill you or destroy your personal life.

The ultimate result of scalable and sustainable businesses is that the owner can step away, and the business will continue. It is the natural result of a well-documented, standardized system. Even if you don't have a written goal to create a business that runs without you, it will happen eventually, if the business is well designed and well run.

To me, the biggest argument against people who poo-poo work-life balance is the fact that it is preached by 99% of all successful people who have ever worked to help others to be successful.

Now, let's look at how you apply this in your business.

42. Why Does Your Business Exist?

I have mentioned in a few places (e.g., Chapters 28 and 34) that your business should exist for a reason. And here's the really good news:

**All small businesses exist to serve
the dreams and goals of the owners.**

That's why we start with your personal goals and how you want to balance your life!

That's not true with big business. Why does a Fortune 500 company exist? To maximize the money in the pockets of the investors. So, if you work at one of those companies, your job is to maximize the investors' profit.

In small business, the business exists to serve the owners' dreams. The owner needs to articulate this, share it with the employees, and make it part of the brand.

Remember what I said in Chapter 28: "Just because you want to do whatever you do, that doesn't make it a business. A business has a reason for existing. If all you want is to 'do' your trade and get money in exchange, that's called a job. Go get a job. But if you want to be in business, you owe your customer more than just trading dollars for hours."

As a business coach over the years, I have worked with business owners who wanted to fund charities, to provide a comfortable retirement for themselves, to buy a second home on the beach, and to save every stray animal in the city. All of these goals are above judgement. You get to create your business to reach your goals. Period.

The Reality of Money

I have found, after working with thousands of business owners, that most of them start their service business for one of three reasons:

1) A horrible former boss (or company) drove them to quit the rat race and go out on their own.
2) They weren't sure what else to do, they were good at "this," and this seemed like a good way to make money.
3) They had an amazing idea to change the world and get rich.

Now, let me be very clear. My very un-scientific observation is that #3 represents less than five percent of all new business adventures—especially in the service industries. Reason #1 represents about eighty percent of all consultants. That leaves reason #2 at just over fifteen percent.

One of my favorite employees over the years ran a business that falls under the #2 rationale. As she explained it to me, her business was something she *could* do. And she saw how she could make money doing it. So, she did it—but she had no passion for it. Her business was literally just a job. It was a way to make money.

Reasons #1 and #3 are far more passionate. Obviously, those who intend to change the world, and make this a better place for all of us, are filled with passion. But so are those who quit a boss and decide to go their own way.

In the big, big picture, I hope you love your job. At least most of the time. This is particularly important when you created the job!

That's why the last chapter matters. You have to have a reason to do what you do. You have to have goals and targets. You have to be able to measure success. That way, you can know when you've achieved it—and you can celebrate.

But let's be realistic about money: We're all in business to make money. Even people who own not-for-profit businesses are after the almighty dollar. One of my favorite markets was always non-profits, simply because they have so much money!

My point is: Once we all acknowledge that we're all in business to make money, then money is no longer the interesting part about the business. Do you need to make a profit of one hundred thousand to feel successful? Two hundred thousand? More?

Most business owners I know work much harder as business owners than they ever would as employees. And—no kidding—most of them make less money than they would as employees.

But there really is such a thing as an "owner's mentality." Business owners won't go home if the client is still in pain. Business owners take out the garbage as well as meet with the clients. Business owners have a vision of the *right way* of delivering service.

See Chapter 4—*The KPE Way*. You have your way. You have your vision about the right way to do this thing you do.

And that vision isn't about money. Yes, you want to make money. Yes, you want to make more money. But your vision about the right way to do what you do is bigger and grander than just making more money.

What is your vision?

Write it down. And if you can't quite put it in words, that's okay. We're not in a hurry here. You have the rest of your life to get this done. Take a stab at it. Write down something. Then you can go back and fine-tune it.

Part of the success model I spell out in *Relax Focus Succeed* is to spend some quiet time every day. This might be prayer or meditation, or simply relaxing in your hot tub and thinking about the day ahead.

Do this for fifteen minutes every day and amazing ideas will flow into your brain. Set the intention on articulating your vision, and it will start to reveal itself to you. Be patient. Do this every day. It might take a week, or a month, or a year.

But eventually, if you work at it, you will be able to boil down your vision to a simple sentence or two. The more you think about it, the clearer it will become.

The more you talk about your vision, the clearer it will become to others. As you describe and explain, you will also answer questions. What about this, or that? And as you answer these questions, you find yourself using the same words over and over to describe your vision.

When you can share your vision with others, it becomes much easier to engage their help. Others will begin to see your vision. A few will fall in love with it. But everyone will understand it, even if it doesn't speak to their personal passion.

And if anyone asks you why your business exists, you'll have an answer.

43. The Culture of Success

We started this discussion in Chapter 22. As you recall, I define culture as *the values and habits of a group.*

I spent a few years as a manager, taking over teams and making them successful. As I look back on the last thirty years, I can honestly say I enjoyed that era a lot—although it was very difficult. It was fulfilling to turn around a culture, once you started to see success. Before that, it was horrible and emotionally draining.

If you are just you and you will never grow a team, then you are responsible for your own attitude and behavior every day. If you're angry or joking, it's up to you to decide how those things affect your company and your reputation.

But if you manage a team of any size, you need to consciously create the culture you want. Just as with your company goals, you need to create a vision of the culture you want. What would your company look like if you had the "right" culture?

Once you have that vision, you can create your culture mission statement. Your mission is the path you need to follow to reach your vision.

You can do a great deal to mold culture through processes and procedures. But the strongest pieces of culture are not found in tangible rules. They're found in human emotions and attitudes. You can't force people to come to work happy, or to be pleased with the decisions you've made.

As a result, culture cannot be something you tackle on a Thursday afternoon and then check the box: Culture—done! No, you build culture with every human interaction, with every hiring decision, with the way you run meetings, with the way you make assignments, and with everything you do every day.

You can never "control" culture, but you can affect it. If you're a parent, you've learned that you cannot control your children. But, if you're consistent and persistent, you can influence them. Eventually (after the teen years are over), your children are very likely to reflect your values and work ethic, because you have modeled it their entire lives.

Molding the culture in your company is very similar. If you come in angry and irritated, barking orders and treating people like garbage, then you can expect that that's how they will treat others. Your clients will see this.

Remember the story in Chapter 12 about the boss who cussed out his employee while Mike and I sat there? We decided instantly, without exchanging a single word, that we would not take them as a client.

Part of our culture is that we only work with people we like. This works its way into our hiring process. A huge part of our team-building takes place at the interview stage. We have several employees interview a candidate and evaluate whether they think they would enjoy working with that person. We actually have an evaluation item about whether they're a good fit for the team.

You cannot force emotions and attitudes on people—but you *can* publicly talk about what you expect. You can put goals and expectations in writing. Remember: One of the great hobbies of all employees is watching the boss!

That sounds a bit ominous, but it's actually good. It makes your job of modeling behavior that much easier. But it also means that you have to "walk the talk" every day.

From time to time, I've worked with companies that have a difficult culture. The boss tolerates abusive managers. Employees see this (they see everything), so they know it does them no good to complain because the bad behavior is already known and accepted.

I can tell you—as a business coach—that this behavior cannot be fixed by a coach. It can only be fixed from the inside, and from the top down. The owner or manager has to *be* the person they want to be seen as. You cannot fake it. And you cannot tolerate bad behavior simply because someone is good at their job.

There is no shortage of talented people on Earth! You don't have to tolerate jerks in your organization.

Success As A Culture

Beyond the general discussion of culture, you can also create a culture that perpetuates the successful habits outlined in this book—or whatever list of Absolutely Unbreakable Rules you create for your company.

As you recall, this list started with a few things written on a piece of paper, pinned to a bulletin board.

- We get paid in advance for everything
- Slow down, get more done
- Do not be interrupt-driven
- Document absolutely everything

. . . and so forth.

As you go about your day, make a point of sharing your rules. Say them often. Say them every time they're relevant. Add them to the bottom of handouts. Post them on the bulletin board.

As I write this final chapter, I'm sitting in the office I share with two employees. There are two white boards. Each has the phrase

"Nothing Happens by Itself"

written across the top. One has a bold declaration, "Branding is everything you do." The other has a smaller note, "Move from un-scalable to scalable." Pinned to one employee's bulletin board is a three-year-old version of the Absolutely Unbreakable Rules.

In other words, we practice what we preach.

I tend to joke around more than the average boss. I don't worry that my sense of humor will undercut my authority. Somewhere along the way, I've created a balance that works for me. I want to enjoy life, so I fill my life with things I enjoy. That includes a positive attitude and a certain amount of humor.

Repeating "the rules" constantly is not a formal, educational endeavor. It's more like a constant, low-level, background atmosphere. You may have grown up with a parent who always had a handful of reliable sayings, like, "It's easier to do it right the first time than to do it over."

That's what you can do in your business. Create an atmosphere in which these rules are not seen as something oppressive that the boss wants us to do, but the true essence of your success.

And, finally, I encourage you to relax about all of this. You have forever to get it right. You don't have to get it perfect on the first day.

I encourage you to create your own list of unbreakable rules. It might be five or ten or twenty-five. But make it yours. Please use this book as a start.

When you've got your one-page list, please send me a copy. I would love to see it. You can find me at

karl@karlpalachuk.com.

Thank you for reading this book. I appreciate any feedback you have.

Bonus Chapter: Just Plain Good Advice

As you may have guessed by now, I love collecting aphorisms. I also collect books filled with great quotations. For me, there is great joy in finding truth in nice, succinct statements.

I also find that exposing myself to all kinds of advice—some of it contradictory—helps me to be more successful. I love mixing up my mental DNA with new thoughts.

You've probably noticed over the years that you hear certain advice again and again. And then, one day, you might read something for the two hundredth time, it suddenly rings true for you. At the right time, under the right circumstances, an old cliché becomes one of the guiding principles of your business (or your life).

So, this chapter is simply a list of all the bits of advice that I decided not to write a chapter about. Maybe someday. But not today.

I hope you find some nuggets here that bring light into your world. If not, well at least you won't waste too much time reading through them.

(Note, also, that I have violated several of these and managed to be successful anyway. So, take it all with a grain of salt.)

A roundup of good advice:

Join a mastermind group.

Over communicate!

Outsource as much as you can.

Determine where fear interferes with your success.

Focus on the highest value tasks at all times.

Focus your business very narrowly (find a niche).

Never do business with friends.

Hire the best help (accountants, attorneys, etc.).

Be at least a little bit better at what you do.

Never hire family.

Be careful about the advice you take.

Be expensive.

Define your ideal client and go after them.

Be yourself! Be authentic.

Never take money out of your retirement accounts.

Believe that no client is indispensable.

Believe that no employee is indispensable.

Believe that you are not indispensable.

Take control of your finances.

Silence means nothing.

It's not about you.

Less drama is good.

More communication is always good.

Problems are never about what they appear to be about. No one gets divorced over socks on the floor.

Something's going to go wrong. Find it, fix it, and move on.

Leave gaps in your day for opportunity to show up.

It's okay to be different. First, you have no choice. Second, revel in it. It's what makes you stand out.

Don't be motivated by fear.

. . . And perhaps the greatest advice I've heard in the last fifteen years:

**"Don't worry what people think about you.
They probably don't."**

I heard that from Arlin Sorensen. He attributes it to his father.

Bonus Chapter: Align Your Services with Client Compliance

By Mike Semel

This chapter was contributed by Mike Semel of Semel Consulting and is copyright © Mike Semel, 2025. www.complianceologist.com

Always Align Your IT Services with Your Client's Compliance Obligations

Delivering IT services while ignoring client compliance is like driving through stop signs. You might get away with it for a while, but eventually, someone gets hurt, you get penalized, and your reputation suffers.

You don't need to be a compliance expert to keep your clients safe, just as you don't need to know the full vehicle and traffic laws to stop at a stop signs. But you do need to deliver services in ways that help clients meet the laws, regulations, and obligations they are bound to follow.

Clients Expect Both Cybersecurity and Compliance

I have performed compliance audits for regulated clients that worked with IT service providers. Many clients failed their assessments because the everyday IT and cybersecurity services they paid for failed to meet their requirements. The clients were angry because they expected their service providers to meet their compliance requirements. Some fired their service providers because the service provider advertised and promised compliant services but didn't deliver them.

Cybersecurity protects data against theft, loss, and unauthorized access. You can deliver cybersecurity services any way you want to.

Compliance is everything someone else makes you do. When you deliver cybersecurity services aligned with your clients' compliance requirements, you help clients avoid incidents, pass audits, and survive investigations. You help them avoid contract cancellations and breach of contract lawsuits.

Audits and investigations require documentation. You can make money by offering documentation-as-a-service by providing clients the monthly reports from your remote management system they will need if they are ever audited or investigated.

By helping clients protect themselves against failing audits, being penalized after incidents, and losing critical contracts or having an insurance claim denied, you can make your work far more valuable—and far harder for competitors to replace.

Avoiding Regulated Clients Is a Mistake

Some IT service providers shy away from regulated clients to "avoid liability." That's a flawed strategy.

- **Every business is regulated.** Even a mom-and-pop store has workforce data it must protect. Avoid compliance altogether and you'll have no clients left.

- **Many industries have heightened requirements**. Healthcare, finance, law firms, accountants, manufacturers, and defense contractors must meet additional rules that extend beyond government regulations. These include ethics requirements, contractual obligations, and cyber insurance mandates.

- **You already have liability protection.** If you use a solid Master Services Agreement (MSA), your liability is limited. Without one, you risk being blamed and sued for everything—even if you weren't at fault. Never provide any service without having a signed MSA.

By leaning into compliance instead of running from it, you strengthen client relationships, stand out from competitors, and often command higher fees.

Laws come from governments. Regulations come from agencies overseeing specific industries. Some major examples:

- **GDPR** – European privacy law
- **HIPAA** – U.S. healthcare privacy and security law
- **GLBA / FTC Safeguards Rule** – Financial institutions
- **NYDFS** Part 500 – New York State financial services
- **Florida Information Protection Act** – State-level privacy law

Some Laws AND Regulations focus on privacy (how data is used and shared). Others focus on *security* (how data is protected). Many combine both. HIPAA, for instance, has a Privacy Rule and a Security Rule. Federal cybersecurity requirements flow down from the federal government to local police departments. HIPAA requirements flow down from healthcare providers and health plans to businesses that support them, including IT professionals.

Industry Requirements

Beyond government regulations, industries impose their own rules. Two examples are:

- **PCI DSS** – Any business that accepts payment cards must comply with the Payment Card Industry Data Security Standard. Requirements vary by volume, process, and breach history.

- **Ethics Rules** – Attorneys and accountants must protect client confidentiality. A data breach caused by negligence can cost them their license.

Contractual Obligations

Contracts can impose the strictest cybersecurity requirements. Violating them can destroy a business overnight if the contract is with a large client or major funding source.

- **Explicit obligations** – Many contracts spell out detailed cybersecurity practices.

- **Hidden clauses** – Defense contracts include a simple DFARS clause number, requiring extensive NIST frameworks and CMMC assessments.

- **Corporate requirements** – Large companies force outside law firms and accountants to follow strict cybersecurity standards. Insurance carriers require a high level of cybersecurity from local agents.

- **Government contracts** – Agencies mandate cybersecurity controls to protect law enforcement or defense data.

The problem? Contracts are often signed without IT input and filed away. Unless you ask clients to review and share clauses, you'll never know the requirements you must align with.

Cyber Insurance

Cyber insurance can cover (among other things) ransom payments, lost profits, forensic and remediation costs, legal fees, reputation recovery. But claims are often denied if businesses fail to implement controls promised on their insurance application or fall into policy exclusions.

Denied claims can mean millions in uncovered costs. Your role is to help clients align IT services with policy requirements.

Be wary if your client asks you to complete their cyber insurance application. The questions ask about cybersecurity for the client's entire business. Limit your answers to the systems you manage and remind the client that they are fully responsible to get answers about the technology you don't manage for them.

Examples of technology not traditionally managed by IT professionals include online ERP, EHR, CRM and other line-of-business applications you don't touch; computer-controlled machines, testing equipment, and medical devices; automated locking, heating, surveillance, and phone systems; and personally owned phones and home computers.

Compliance Stacks Up

Most businesses must comply with **multiple requirements simultaneously**. For example, a doctor in New York who accepts Medicare and credit cards, and carries cyber insurance, must follow:

- HIPAA (federal healthcare law)
- NY SHIELD Act (state privacy law)
- Medicare contractual cybersecurity requirements
- PCI DSS (payment card security)
- Cyber insurance obligations

This doctor can be audited at any time for any of them. If they fail an audit or investigation, they'll likely blame their IT service provider. That's a risk—but also a **huge opportunity.**

By aligning your services with frameworks like CIS Controls, NIST Cybersecurity Framework (CSF), or NIST SP 800-171 (for defense contractors under CMMC), you help clients meet multiple requirements without learning every detail of every regulation. And you protect yourself by showing you delivered a "reasonable" program. If you just 'wing it' with your own program and let your client decline services, you open yourself up to liability.

Action Steps for IT Service Providers

1. Embrace Compliance. Don't avoid it. If you're smart enough to manage IT and cybersecurity, you can learn how to integrate compliance into your services.

2. Lock Down Your Master Service Agreement (MSA). Your Master Services Agreement should:
- Require clients to disclose all compliance requirements
- State that you don't guarantee full compliance coverage
- Absolve you of liability for client responsibilities, including implementing the cybersecurity you recommend and managing their technology that you don't touch
- Limit liability to direct damages, with reasonable caps
- Be customized for you by an MSP-focused attorney familiar with your company

3. Identify Requirements. Work with prospects and clients to uncover all obligations, including laws and regulations, industry requirements, contractual clauses, and cyber insurance policies.

4. Learn Key Requirements. Examples of critical items you should learn and follow include:
- PCI DSS requires card systems on separate network segments.
- HIPAA and others require risk assessments and ongoing risk management.
- Most regulations require access logs, log reviews, and log retention for all access to regulated data, even on local devices
- Regulations often flow down—HIPAA requires Business Associates (including you) to comply.

5. Deliver Services That Align. Best practices that map to most regulations include encrypting all devices and portable media, enforcing multifactor authentication (MFA) everywhere, regularly validating user accounts to cut off former employees, backing up all critical data and testing recoverability, and logging user access as well as reviewing and retaining those logs.

6. Use a Shared Responsibility Matrix (SRM). Include an SRM in your MSA and Scope of Work. Clearly separate client vs. provider responsibilities. For example, client responsibility includes authorizing new users and informing you when employees leave while provider responsibility includes implementing secure access and removing users when notified. Make sure the SRM states you're not responsible for any security in client-managed systems or cloud services you don't manage.

7. Back Words With Action. Don't market "compliance services" unless you actually deliver them. Too many MSPs advertise HIPAA, FTC, and CMMC compliance but their clients fail basic audits. Clients feel misled, fire providers, and sometimes pursue legal action.

The Bottom Line

Compliance isn't optional. It's everywhere—laws, ethics, contracts, insurance—and clients expect you to help them navigate it. If you lean into compliance, you:

- Win more clients in regulated industries
- Charge higher fees for the same cybersecurity services your competitors offer
- Deepen relationships and reduce churn
- Protect yourself with documented alignment to frameworks and contracts

Compliance is not extra work. It's smarter work. Compliance isn't different from cybersecurity. It's implementing cybersecurity according to rules, like driving according to traffic laws. By delivering services that are both secure and compliant, you protect clients from harm and yourself from being blamed later.

Compliance is the difference between being just another IT provider—and being indispensable.

Acronyms and Alphabet Soup

- CIS Controls – Center for Internet Security Controls.
- CMMC – Cybersecurity Maturity Model Certification.
- DFARS – Defense Federal Acquisition Regulation Supplement.
- FTC – Federal Trade Commission
- GDPR – General Data Protection Regulation, a regulation by the European Union and separately by the UK
- GLBA / FTC Safeguards Rule –Gramm-Leach-Bliley Act is a U.S. federal law governing banks, insurance, and investment financial institutions. The FTC Safeguards Rule is a part of GLBA, mandating how non-banking financial institutions protect customer information.
- HIPAA – Health Insurance Portability and Accountability Act.
- NIST – National Institute of Standards and Technology.
- NYDFS Part 500 – New York State Department of Financial Services Cybersecurity Regulation.
- PCI DSS – Payment Card Industry Data Security Standard.

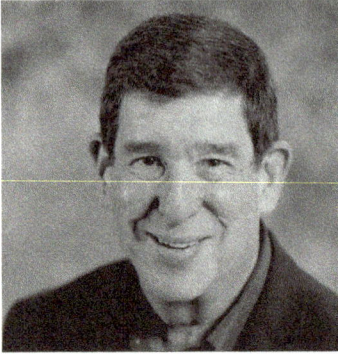

Mike Semel 'The Complianceologist' is recognized as a thought leader in the IT, compliance, and business continuity industries. He is the President of Semel Consulting, focused on regulatory compliance and comprehensive Business Continuity planning. He has owned or managed MSP companies for over 30 years; served as Chief Information Officer (CIO) for a hospital and a K-12 school district; and managed operations at an online backup company. Mike is the only expert who consulted with CompTIA on the original Security Trustmark (2008), the Security Trustmark Plus (2014), and the Cybersecurity Trustmark (2023). He is the best-selling author of How to Avoid HIPAA Headaches. Mike is a CMMC Certified Assessor (CCA), CMMC Certified Professional (CCP), CMMC Registered Practitioner (RP), Certified Security Compliance Specialist, ISC2 Certified Governance Risk Compliance, Disaster Recovery Institute Certified Business Continuity Professional & Certified Cyber Resilience Professional, Certified HIPAA Security Professional, and Certified Health IT Specialist. Mike can be reached at mike@semelconsulting.com.

Resources and References

Boorstein, Sylvia. *Don't Just Do Something, Sit There.* HarperOne. 1996.

Canfield, Jack, Leslie Hewitt, and Mark Victor Hansen. *The Power of Focus.* Random. 2001.

The Cruise Industry News Quarterly in 1999. John McNeece.

Federal Reserve. *2018 Survey of Household Economics and Decision Making.* https://www.federalreserve.gov/publications/files/2017-report-economic-well-being-us-households-201805.pdf.

Gerber, Michael. *The E-Myth Revisited.* Harper. 2004.

Google.com. Search: "Conscious Competence."

Google.com. Search: "Dunning-Kruger Effect."

Goulston, Dana J., and Karl W. Palachuk. *Project Management in Small Business - How to Deliver Successful, Profitable Projects on Time with Your Small Business Clients.* Great Little Book. 2014.

Hsieh, Tony. *Delivering Happiness: A Path to Profits, Passion, and Purpose.* Grand Central Publishing. 2013.

Michalowicz, Mike. *Profit First: Transform Your Business from a Cash-Eating Monster to a Money-Making Machine.* Portfolio. 2017.

The New Yorker. July 5, 1993. Cartoon: "On the Internet, no one knows you're a dog."

Packard, David. *The HP Way.* Harper. 2006. See also www.hpalumni.org/hp_way.htm.

Palachuk, Karl W. *Relax Focus Succeed: Balance Your Personal and Professional Lives and Be More Successful in Both*. Revised Edition. Great Little Book. 2013.

Palachuk, Karl W. *The Network Documentation Workbook*. SMB Nation. 2005.

Palachuk, Karl W. *Managed Services in a Month*, 3rd edition. Great Little Book. 2018.

Palachuk, Karl W. *Cloud Services in a Month*. Great Little Book. 2018.

Palachuk, Karl W. and Manuel Palachuk. *The Network Migration Workbook*, 2nd edition. Great Little Book. 2009.

Palachuk, Karl W. *The Managed Services Operations Manual*—four volume set. Great Little Book. 2014.

Palachuk, Karl. YouTube channel: www.youtube.com/smallbizthoughts.

Plato. *The Phaedrus*.

Quote Investigator: https://quoteinvestigator.com/2011/07/28/ford-faster-horse/

Schwerdtfeger, Patrick. *Webify Your Business, Internet Marketing Secrets for the Self-Employed*. Lulu. 2009.

Shakespeare, William. *Hamlet*.

Sinek, Simon. *Start with Why*. Portfolio. 2011.

Strauss, Robert S. Washington (DC) Star-News. December 1974. (Source for quote, "Success is a little like wrestling a gorilla. You don't quit when you're tired. You quit when the gorilla is tired.")

Tracy, Brian. Everything you can find.

Tracy, Brian. *How the Best Leaders Lead: Proven Secrets to Getting the Most Out of Yourself and Others.* AMACOM. 2010.

Other Resources from Karl W. Palachuk

www.RelaxFocusSucceed.com
Information on the book, of course. Articles, blog posts, a collection of Karl's favorite pithy quotations, and a monster recommended reading list. Sign up for the Relax Focus Succeed™ monthly newsletter!

www.SmallBizQuickstart.com
This site is dedicated to the book *The Small Biz Quickstart Workbook*—a great resource for new business owners and those who are working to quit their job and start a business.

www.KarlPalachuk.com
This is our primary site for business advice, speaking, coaching, technical topics, managed services, running your business, and more.

About the Author

Karl W. Palachuk is a speaker, author, and coach who has trained technology consultants and business owners all over the world. He's the author of more than twenty-five books on business processes, work-life balance, book publishing, project management, and technology consulting.

Karl has been an IT Consultant since 1995 and is one of the pioneers of the managed services business model. He is also a business coach, and the founder of the Small Biz Thoughts Technology Community.

Karl has owned several small businesses, including two very successful IT consulting companies, a book publishing company, an online community, and an online training company. He loves to travel, and normally manages to add some personal time to every trip – so he can experience the cities he visits.

For more than a decade, Karl has restructured his life and his business so they are one hundred percent compatible and support each other. His personal mission is to "Inspire success through a balance of serving myself and serving others." All of his companies share a related vision: "To make every small business a successful small business."

If Karl ever goes missing, he's probably on a beach somewhere—writing his next book.

Please contact him at karl@karlpalachuk.com.

Index

A

B

C

KERNAN CONSULTING

THINKING OF BUYING OR SELLING YOUR BUSINESS?

➤ **Sell-Side Representation**

➤ **Strategic Advisory & Valuations**

➤ **Buy-Side Representation**

We specialize in M&A and strategic advisory services, leveraging deep market knowledge to support business acquisitions, sales, and valuations. Our experienced team committed to delivering exceptional execution and service to meet our client's strategic goals.

LET'S CONNECT!

James Kernan
Kernan Consulting
402-493-5550 X101

"Being an MSP can feel like being on an island. ASCII makes sure you are never stranded."

Karl Palachuk, *ASCII Group Member Since 2005*

Established in 1984, The ASCII Group has been bringing MSPs together across North America — offering resources, relationships, and support that help members feel part of something bigger.

Join the #1 trusted community for MSPs.

Use promo code *KARL* to receive an additional membership bonus.

800-394-2724
lynn@ascii.com
www.ascii.com

ascii
the ascii group, inc.
MEMBER

THE PREMIER IT
COMMUNITY

"Mike Semel is the number one consultant you need to go to for compliance education and implementation at any level. **When I think compliance, I think Mike Semel.**"

— Karl W. Palachuk, author and coach

→ ANOTHER UNBREAKABLE RULE
Your clients expect your services to meet their compliance requirements.

→ EVERY BUSINESS IS REGULATED
Don't get blamed. Don't get fired. Don't get sued. You don't need to become a compliance expert to deliver compliant services.

→ COMPLIANCE REFERRAL PROGRAM
Refer clients to us. Get a referral fee. We don't compete with you. HIPAA, CMMC, FTC, GLBA, PCI, NIST, Business Continuity Plan

SEMEL
CONSULTING

www.semelconsulting.com

COMPLIANCE TRAINING FOR IT PROS

COMPLIANCEOLOGIST
www.complianceologist.com